The Civil War:
The Nantucket Experience

"All that was left, 1930"—Surviving members of Thomas M. Gardner Post 207, Grand Army of the Republic: Josiah Fitch Murphey, James H. Barrett, James H. Wood.

The
Nantucket
Experience

Including the Memoirs
of Josiah Fitch Murphey

Rob. F. Mooney

Richard F. Miller and Robert F. Mooney

Wesco Publishing
Nantucket, Massachusetts
1994

Wesco Publishing
P.O. Box 1540
Nantucket, Massachusetts 02554

ISBN 0-9627851-1-3

Composed in Perpetua by
Graphic Arts Consortium,
Nantucket, Massachusetts.
Printed and bound by Thomson Shore, Dexter, Michigan.
The paper is Joy White Offset, an acid-free sheet.
Printed in the United States of America.

CONTENTS

v

LIST OF ILLUSTRATIONS

Cover illustrations:
Josiah Fitch Murphey in 1862.
Photograph courtesy of Francis W. Pease
View of Nantucket Town from Brant Point, 1875.
Photograph: Nantucket Historical Association

Frontispiece:
"All that was left, 1930"—Surviving members of Thomas M. Gardner
Post 207, Grand Army of the Republic: Josiah Fitch Murphey,
James H. Barrett, James H. Wood.
Photograph: Nantucket Historical Association

Illustrations following page 52:

1 Leander F. Alley, 1834–62. Here in uniform of a private, he was
   commissioned second lieutenant in the field and was killed at
   Fredericksburg.
   Photograph: Probably 1861, Nantucket Historical Association

2 Josiah Fitch Murphey, having recovered from typhoid fever
   contracted after the battle of Fredericksburg.
   Photograph: 1863, courtesy of Francis W. Pease

3 Brevet Major General George Nelson Macy, 1837–75, Nantucket's
   highest ranking officer in the Civil War.
   Photograph: Ca. 1865, courtesy of Houghton Library, Harvard University

Authors' Preface

CONCEIVED AS A MURAL, THE CIVIL WAR is so vast a canvas that the temptation is to stand back and view the whole from the perspective of a Lincoln or a Lee, a Grant or a Jefferson Davis. While the view from the Oval Office or the general's headquarters may have a certain appeal, an invaluable aspect is found in the detailed life of the small communities and usually obscure people who waged the war; paid the taxes to support it; and suffered, died, or agonized over the fate of loved ones, hundreds of miles away, who were engaged in the great cause.

This is the story of the island community of Nantucket and some of its men at war during the greatest crisis in American history. The Nantucket story must include that of the 20th Massachusetts Volunteer Infantry, one of the most famous units in the Army of the Potomac. More Nantucket men—eighty—served in Company I of the 20th than in any other single regiment, and often the anxieties and emotions of Nantucketers during the war years rested with the fate of the 20th Massachusetts.

Because of the scope of the war, the present work cannot be considered a comprehensive history of Nantucket's involvement in it. Island men also served in the navy—some with Farragut, others on blockade ships and on the western waterways. Nantucketers served in other Union regiments, and, due to the wide dispersal of the nation's population in the prewar years, some Nantucketers saw service in the western theater. Nantucket's small but patriotic, *and free*, African-American community sent their sons and husbands to serve—in the navy at first and, later, in the colored regiments of the army. They rendered honorable service and returned to become respected veterans. All these men deserve recognition and future attention; the authors regret that their focus in the present work bars inclusion of their stories.

Recognizing these deficiencies, the authors have tried to present the impact of the Civil War on a small town and its people, the personal story of the common soldier and why he went to war, and the spirit that produced uncommon valor among common people at a time of national crisis. Any merit this work has belongs to those people, and the authors take full responsibility for any defects that may be apparent in presenting their history.

Acknowledgments

IT CAN FAIRLY BE SAID THAT WRITING THE HISTORY of a community requires a community effort, and the authors have certainly found this to be true in completing *The Civil War: The Nantucket Experience.*

The Nantucket Atheneum, Nantucket's historic public library, is a treasure trove of island history. It was there that the people of Nantucket gathered to rally for the Cause, and it is the repository for original and microfilmed copies of wartime numbers of the *Weekly Mirror* and the Nantucket *Inquirer,* and postwar issues of the short-lived Nantucket *Journal,* in which were found much of the root material for this book. The authors are indebted to the entire Atheneum staff, especially Lee Rand Burne, whose unstinting research efforts and scholarly attention have enriched the work.

Nantucket Historical Association staff, especially archivist Jacqueline Haring and librarians Amy Rokicki and Betsy Tyler, generously gave their time and expertise in helping us to mine the depths of the association's rich archives. Thanks are also due to Peter MacGlashan, the NHA's audio-visual curator, whose preservation efforts have ensured that images of Nantucket and its people will be on hand for future generations. Doug Burch, editor of the NHA's quarterly *Historic Nantucket,* was also helpful.

The late Edouard A. Stackpole, dean of Nantucket historians, contributed greatly to this work. His personal reminiscences of Nantucket's Civil War veterans were invaluable, but more so was his collection of war memorabilia, assembled over a lifetime and now stored in the Research Center at the Peter Foulger Museum.

The authors are grateful to Mary Havemeyer Beman, proprietor of Mitchell's Book Corner, for professional advice and encouragement. Nantucket's town clerk, Rebecca Lohmann, assisted greatly in accessing town records that were essential to compiling the roster. Thanks to Allen Dean Cummings for his assistance in creating the computer program that vastly simplified the collection of data for the roster.

Direct descendants of Nantucket men who fought in the war keep the memory of their ancestors fresh, and have provided access to family artifacts and correspondence. Francis Pease, great-grandson of Josiah Fitch Murphey, and Charles "Jack" Gardner, great-grandson of Elisha Pope Fearing Gardner, shared with the authors photographs, books, documents, and family legends of its own Civil War experience.

Appreciation is expressed to Leslie Morris, curator of manuscripts at Harvard University's Houghton Library, and James E. Fahey, archivist at the Commonwealth of Massachusetts' Military Division History Research and Museum at Natick. Each is responsible for different and priceless collections, which both cheerfully placed at our disposal.

A special note of thanks is due our invaluable editor, Elizabeth Oldham, who has left her mark on other books and was especially helpful in producing this work.

Finally, the authors wish to express their profound thanks for the love, patience, and perseverance of Alyson Miller and Betty Mooney, both of whom were temporarily widowed by a war that had supposedly ended 129 years ago. It is to them that this book is dedicated, in the hope of making partial amends for the long absences of their devoted husbands.

Richard F. Miller
Robert F. Mooney

Nantucket, Massachusetts
September 1994

I Nantucket During the Civil War

ety of Friends was split by religious disputes, resulting in the unseemly spectacle of publicly feuding Quaker factions. As the Quaker influence diminished, the mainstream Congregationalists, Unitarians, and Methodists expanded their base on Nantucket, eventually constructing magnificent churches that remain architecturally significant to this day. Within a few years, the social and political scene on Nantucket changed completely.

BY THE CRITICAL YEARS OF MID-CENTURY, the island of Nantucket, though economically moribund, was politically alive and concerned about national issues. Turning from the traditional isolation and pacifism that had characterized the island during the reign of the Quaker oligarchy, Nantucketers became full-fledged northern patriots, debating the future of slavery and dedicating themselves to the preservation of the Union. The public attitude was the result of increased contact with mainland thinkers and speakers who came to speak at the Atheneum and the influence of the local press, which contributed to the islanders' new awareness and growing national consciousness.

Both weekly newspapers, the *Inquirer* and the *Mirror*, were strongly Republican in their editorials. The *Inquirer* supported the election of Abraham Lincoln in 1860, while the *Mirror* subscribed to most of the principles of the Chicago Platform.* The *Mirror* did not endorse Lincoln because of its longstanding policy against endorsing candidates of any stripe. Prior to the outbreak of the war, it pictured the secessionist movement as the work of misguided southern firebrands who were leading loyal Southerners astray. Once the war erupted, the papers were quick to shift to patriotic enthusiasm, urging the young men from the depressed island to find excitement and adventure by enlisting in a short and glorious war against a small band of traitors whose only aim was the destruction of the nation.

---

*The Chicago Platform of 1860 pledged the party to resist the expansion of slavery into free states, denounced the violence of John Brown's Raid, supported liberal wages for working men, and opposed nativist restrictions on immigration.

Both newspapers were opposed to the principle of slavery, and most Nantucketers supported that position. However, both newspapers and general island opinion were prepared to accept the institution of slavery where it existed, but not its expansion, for the sake of preserving the Union. In 1860, Nantucketers shared an attitude common to virtually all northern communities. Preservation of the Union, not slavery, was the main issue in the presidential election of 1860.

On election day, November 6, 1860, 599 Nantucket voters, all men, turned up at the polls, casting 420 votes for Lincoln, 76 for Bell; 61 for Breckenridge, and 32 for Stephen Douglas. Decisively rejected were John Bell, representing an untenable compromise with the South; Stephen Douglas, representing the old order of appeasing southern interests; and John Breckenridge, the most pro-southern candidate of the four. The 420 votes for Lincoln were votes for the Union. Not surprisingly, the votes for Congress and the state ticket made it a Republican landslide. So excited were the voters over the results, they sent the yacht *Wide Awake* over to Hyannis on Tuesday evening to announce the Nantucket vote, and more important, to obtain the results of the national election.

The *Wide Awake* returned with the results, but it wasn't until the steamer arrived on Wednesday, November 7, that the town celebrated the official news. A torchlight procession of more than 150 persons gathered in the lower square on Main Street. Under the direction of Chief Marshall Charles Wood and Captain Daniel Russell, four engine companies and the Nantucket Brass Band band led the parade up Main Street, stopping before the Republican headquarters where three rockets were fired into the evening air and a 100-gun salute was raised for the President-elect.

Along the route of the procession, the marchers stopped several times at the homes of Nantucket dignitaries, who had illuminated their homes with gaslights and displayed pictures of Abraham Lincoln. After innumerable cheers and salutes, the parade returned to the square, bearing banners that read, "We march to the music of the Union," "The mudsills have arisen," and "All up for Lincoln, Hamblin and Andrew," the latter being Republican Governor John A. Andrew of Massachusetts. Even their political opponents admired the show, and, as the Democratic epistler to the *Mirror* phrased it, "yielded with excellent grace to the irresistible power of destiny."

A week later, the local *Mirror* editorialized upon the impending threat of disunion:

> The hot blood of our brethren at the South seems fairly to effervesce at the news of the recent national election. The advocates of disunion, for secession is no less than disunion, are unwilling to wait for Mr. Lincoln to assume his seat and to indicate his policy...The Republican party is not homogeneous...nowhere in its political manifestoes do we find any expression which warrants the idea that slavery is to be interfered with in the States where it now exists, only that the area of slavery should not be extended...Now is the time for moderate counsels and moderate words. Let us seek for peace, and things that make for peace.

Toward the end of the year, the papers echoed the sentiment that the South was making a big mistake as it headed toward secession but that the current tension, nonetheless, stemmed from extremists on both sides. The *Mirror* editorialized: "The North as a whole does not look upon the South with unfriendly regard. The great majority of our people appreciate the circumstances of their slaveholding brethren, born to a troublesome inheritance, which they cannot cast off."

The *Inquirer*'s editorial of December 26, 1860, doubtless spoke for a majority of Nantucketers when it presciently declared, months before Fort Sumter:

> The South seems determined not to understand the North. . . . The South is woefully, and we almost fear, fatally mistaken. The large majority of the sober people here have nothing but love for the people of the South. . . . We speak now of the mass of the people. We say nothing, to be sure, of the wild handful of fanatics, some with hearts bigger than their heads, and some with neither hearts nor heads, who go about seeking whom they may devour. . . . From such we withdraw ourselves. We do not like the institution of Slavery but will permit it and sustain it as far as the constitution requires us to, because our fathers agreed with your fathers that it should be so. But be not deceived. . . . When every peace offering has been refused . . . then the great army of those who sympathize with the Southern States will be found shoulder to shoulder to save the Union. Thousands upon thousands would then rush to the Federal Standard. We say to the South, don't mistake our silence and our concessions. We mean them, and we want you in the Union; but when you try to cut the silver cord, then you will find that we love our country more.

Despite the hopeful plea of the editorials, the year ended with the realization that South Carolina had passed the Ordinance of Secession and was already making demands on the Federal government to turn over its property. Something would have to be done about Fort Sumter in Charleston Harbor. It appeared that the national government would be unable to act until President Lincoln was sworn in.

The inauguration of Lincoln in March 1861, preceded by the secession of more southern states, brought the *Mirror*'s comment:

> It is also manifest that the President does not mean to coerce. Meantime, in the loyal States, men are calculating the value of union, or they are becoming reconciled to actual disunion. It is absurd to suppose that the seceded States will return to the union as it was five months ago. . . . The curse of slavery lies on us all; not alone on the South, but on us. The fathers have eaten sour grapes and the children's teeth are set on edge.

On Nantucket, the islanders knew that momentous national events were pending, but they had no idea of what the outcome would be. The first news came one afternoon in April of 1861. A large crowd had gathered in the lower square of Main Street, anxiously awaiting the news from the mainland port of Hyannis. All eyes looked to the newsline of the steamship, as they had for years. The steamer *Island Home* had initiated the practice of flying a special signal from its flagstaff to alert the community to impending important news.

Expecting daily to see that signal, the townspeople placed a lookout atop the Customs House, now the Pacific Club, on Lower Main Street. Peering through his long glass, he first caught sight of the ship approaching the island. Then he watched steadily until he sighted the signal and shouted to the crowd in the street below.

Captain Joseph Hamblin, standing at the corner of Main and Washington streets, announced the news Nantucket had expected: "I guess they have fired the first shot!"

"AND THE WAR CAME," as President Lincoln would note later.

Almost overnight, and improbably, the men on the peaceful Quaker island of Nantucket established a militia, the "Island Guard," and it became the pride of the community. The men of the Island Guard were to be the nucleus of Nantucket's deeply tragic yet valorous connection with one of the Civil War's legendary regiments—the 20th Massachusetts Volunteer Infantry. To some extent, the eighty Nantucketers who passed through the ranks of the regiment would define the island's perception of the war. And that perception would be bloodstained soon enough at places called Ball's Bluff, the Peninsula, Second Manassas, Antietam, Fredericksburg, Chancellorsville, Gettysburg, the Wilderness, Spotsylvania, Petersburg, and, finally, Appomattox.

1861: The War Begins
The 20th Massachusetts Volunteer Infantry

THEY CALLED IT THE HARVARD REGIMENT. The Commonwealth of Massachusetts was deeply committed to the Union cause during the Civil War, and it had a special reason to be proud of the 20th Massachusetts Volunteer Infantry. Although men of the regiment were all volunteers, recruited mostly from the towns of eastern Massachusetts, almost all the officers were graduates of Harvard College. Many of the young men of the Class of 1861 were eager to volunteer for service in the Union Army, and with the patriotic spirit prevailing in the Commonwealth, Harvard men were never refused commissions.

On June 27, 1861, Massachusetts Governor John Albion Andrew appointed Colonel William R. Lee, an engineer who had studied at West Point with Jefferson Davis, to take command of the 20th Massachusetts, and further authorized him to appoint his own officers. As a result, appointments included some of the most famous names in Massachusetts history: Lieutenant Colonel Francis Winthrop Palfrey, Major Paul Joseph Revere (grandson of the midnight rider), Adjutant Charles Lawrence Pierson, Captain William Francis Bartlett, Captain Caspar Crowninshield, Lieutenant Henry Livermore Abbott, Lieutenant Charles F. Cabot, Lieutenant Norwood Penrose Hallowell, and Lieutenant Oliver Wendell Holmes, Jr.

The regiment was ordered into training at Camp Massasoit, a new camp laid out on the banks of the Neponset River in the town of Readville, near Dedham. The site was selected for its good water supply and railroad connections to Boston and Providence. The summer of 1861 was devoted to recruiting and drilling the new recruits, developing the military skills of the young officers, and molding the new men of the 20th Massachusetts into a fighting force.

The strength of the volunteer army of 1861 depended upon vigorous recruitment efforts, and one of the tasks assigned to the junior officers of the regiment was the recruiting of volunteers from nearby communities. Lieutenant George Nelson Macy, a twenty-three-year-old native of Nantucket, soon emerged as a leader in the effort, and his persuasive talents brought a distinctive cast of characters to the regiment. On his first weekend leave from Camp Massasoit, Macy went home on recruiting duty and returned on July 21 with twenty-three Nantucket men in tow, eager to be mustered in. He continued his weekly recruiting forays with repeated success. Macy's Nantucket men were all volunteers and eager for adventure, fearing only that the war would end before they could get into action. Full of high spirits and civic pride, the local nature of the recruits reflected their rural and independent background. By the time the regiment was ready to break camp, there were eighty men from Nantucket enrolled in Company I of the 20th Massachusetts Volunteer Infantry.

Faced with a world of adventure, the promise of travel and excitement, and the dismal prospects of remaining at home, the boys of Nantucket were quick to volunteer for the war. Like the boys in other towns, North and South, they preferred the communal nature of the companies and regiments where entire units were often recruited from single towns and counties, reflecting hometown loyalties. They liked to serve under officers and top sergeants whom they knew and respected, men who talked their own language. Thus, the new regiments combined civic pride with national patriotism. And so they went to war.

The commander of Company I was Captain William "Frank" Bartlett, a Harvard man who had great military promise. He selected George Nelson Macy as his first lieutenant and Henry Livermore Abbott, of

Lowell, as his second lieutenant. The two young men were from different backgrounds, yet they soon became close friends and comrades in arms. Macy was born in Nantucket, and after graduation from Nantucket schools found work as a bank clerk in Boston before earning his commission at the age of twenty-three. Abbott was the son of a prominent family, a graduate of Harvard with the Class of 1861, and was commissioned at the age of nineteen. Their careers with the regiment became a paradigm of life with the Army of the Potomac.

Each time a new batch of Nantucket men came in, Lieutenant Oliver Wendell Holmes, Jr., prayed he would not get them in his company. Many New England men displayed a Yankee contempt for authority, but the farmers and seamen from Nantucket seemed more insolent than most. When the day's drill was over, the men simply departed, without leave, across the plain to the tavern in Mill Village and got thoroughly drunk. If the new recruits were not getting drunk, they were off swimming in the Neponset River. When the young Lieutenant Holmes reprimanded them, he was bluntly asked why a man shouldn't go where he pleased when his day's work was done, and spend his own money without asking leave of any goddam officer.*

The Nantucket men were also noted for their fine physical condition. During an era when the mustering officer sometimes found that almost a third of the recruits were physically unfit for the service, the Nantucket farmers and sailors were found to be healthy fellows. One husky specimen, William P. Kelley, so impressed Surgeon Bryant during his physical examination that the doctor whistled in admiration and called Lieutenant Holmes to look over his newest prize.

Although the full complement of a regiment was a thousand men, the 20th Massachusetts never attained it. The urgency of the war demanded immediate manpower, and the regiment numbered only 750 men, with thirty-five officers. Nor was there time for the formal mustering of the regiment on Boston Common, as was the tra-

---

*This anecdote was related in Catherine Drinker Bowen's *Yankee from Olympus: Justice Holmes and His Family*, Atlantic Monthly Press, 1944.

dition; so without ceremony, and with all too little training, the Nantucket boys went off to war.

ON OCTOBER 21, 1861, THE 20TH MASSACHUSETTS, Company I in particular, played a prominent part in the battle of Ball's Bluff, Virginia, one of the Union Army's early disasters, and one that revealed many defects in the Federal command.

Commanded by the militarily inept Edward D. Baker, Senator from Oregon and a personal friend of Lincoln, Union forces crossed to the Virginia side of the Potomac fifty miles north of Washington. The intent was to capture Leesburg, which was thought to be lightly defended by the Confederate Army. The rebels turned out to be numerous and skilfully commanded, and the Federals were driven back to the river bank, where few boats were available to transport thousands of panicked Union soldiers.

Nantucket Private Benjamin H. Whitford, in a letter to his wife, wrote a lengthy description of the battle that was reprinted in the Nantucket *Mirror*:

As soon as I saw the boats I felt that we were bound on a perilous expedition, but the order was forward, and on we went. Five hundred of the Mass. 15th preceded us and we found them drawn up on the heights on our arrival. On the Virginia side where we landed, a high bluff rises almost perpendicular some 75 or 100 feet, with only a narrow path at its base and winding up its side. . . . On the top of this bluff we found an old clearing of about 40 acres surrounded by woods on all sides. . . . Col Lee was with us. Sergeant Riddle went with one party of five and I went with another; I found no pickets in the direction I took, but Riddle soon fell in with one who fired on him, wounding his right forearm; whether he will lose it or not, I cannot tell. Five more companies of our regiment were landed by 12 M (noon). Col Baker took command and posted us on the verge of the cliff, our flanks resting on the woods.

About 2 PM the enemy opened fire on us before we saw them, and a perfect hurricane of bullets rushed over our heads and around us. . . . Our reinforcements arrived slowly and theirs came up by the thousands. . . . At this time, three shots fell between Capt. Bartlett and myself, evidently aimed at him from the tree-tops, and I discovered the fellow by the smoke from his gun. Capt. B gave me leave to go and pick him off, which I did. In loading his piece he exposed a portion of his body; I fired and down he came, a dead man. . . . The battle raged until night. . . . We were now exposed to a terrible fire from the front and both flanks and were compelled to retire before a vastly superior force to the front of the cliff. I had fired all but one charge and that was in my gun. . . . When the order to retire to the river was given, I jumped over the rocks at the top of the bluff and halted out of the way of stray bullets. While standing at that place, Edward Orpin of Nantucket jumped over at the same place and quietly informed me that a man was aiming at me from behind a tree only 10 or 12 feet from me. I dropped just as he fired. He then fired his revolver at Orpin as he went tumbling down the cliff, saying, "Run, you son of a bitch!" I then raised my rifle, and with my last shot sent him to his long account. . . . When I arrived I found that Orpin had reported me shot dead through the head, and I had several holes in my clothes. Captain Bartlett and the Colonel sat together, the dead and wounded lining the bank. I went up to my Capt. and asked, "What are the orders?" The reply was, "Swim or surrender."

It is perhaps not surprising that when Benjamin Whitford's enlistment expired three years hence, he would reenlist, but as a hospital steward, a noncombatant.

Some of the officers behaved well under fire. Captain William Bartlett, commanding Company I of the 20th Massachusetts, walked about calmly under fire, joking with Lieutenant George N. Macy who was lying on the grass, saying he should be careful or he would get his new coat stained. On the bank, with the rebels firing from the bluffs into the crowd of panicked Yankees, Lieutenant Macy stripped off his clothes (except for his hat, which carried a miniature of his fiancée), and swam the river to find more boats, an action that won him an early promotion to captain.

On November 1, Captain Bartlett wrote a letter to Lieutenant Macy's father, George W. Macy, in which he provided the sad accounting of Nantucket's dead, wounded, and missing as a result of the battle:

Camp Benton, Nov 1st 1861

Mr. George W. Macy: I take the liberty of addressing you, sir, to ask that you will say to those relations and friends of the killed and missing men of my company, belonging to Nantucket, that they have the sweet consolation of knowing that they died like heroes and brave men; that they fell, fighting for the honor and liberties of a country, which will remember them with a tear of gratitude as long as her history shall be written.

George G. Worth was one of the best men in the regiment, honest, open-hearted and brave, and it was a severe blow to me to hear that he was among the missing. He was probably shot while crossing the river, after fighting bravely through the day until ordered to retreat.

Mr. Samuel Lowell is not dead, I hope, but a prisoner. He went up the bank of the river with me, and wandered off with two or three men to surrender themselves as prisoners, as none of us expected to escape. He was always so quiet and obliging that he won the respect of every man in the company, by whom he was always addressed as Mr. Lowell.

Albert Kelley was unhurt when last seen on the bank of the river. He was probably taken prisoner with the others.

Albert Stackpole has since died of his wounds. He bore his sufferings with courage and patience. We buried him as a soldier on Sunday last, Oct. 27th. A small inscription marks his grave, near the main road leading to the Ferry. I cannot close without alluding to the honor which is due all your townsmen in the last disastrous battle. Nantucket may well be proud of such sons. They all acted the part of brave men fighting in their country's cause, and never yielded their ground until driven back by superior numbers, and then only at the orders of their commanding officer.

George C. Pratt is in the hospital, wounded, where he receives every attention that can conduce his comfort. He is getting along finely and is in excellent spirits.

John W. Summerhayes was slightly wounded in the hand, but is now entirely well, and is devoting his attentions to the wounded men in the hospital.

To mention those of the company who acted with especial bravery, would be but to give you the whole roll call. Allow me to congratulate you on Lieut. Macy's conduct and safety.

I remain. your obedient servant, W.F. Bartlett, Capt. Co. I, 20th Regiment, Mass. Vol.

1862

PATRIOTISM RAN HIGH IN NANTUCKET at the start of 1862. The Reverend Isaac C. White of the First Congregational Society sermonized on the national crisis and the cause of the present troubles: "Sin is the cause, and the particular form of sin is slavery." It was a war of right against wrong. When the smoke of the conflict had been swept away, a brighter sun would shed its beams. The preacher was patriotic and optimistic.

The members of the Dramatic Club presented an evening of entertainment and comedy in the Atheneum Hall in January, the proceeds going to benefit the Massachusetts volunteers. The chorus included "The Star Spangled Banner," "The Child of the Regiment," and "'It Is Sweet to Die for One's Country." Citizens were urged to write and send newspapers to the boys in the service; messages that "will be a great moral safeguard; and will weave new chords of filial affection."

The *Mirror* editorialized on January 25, 1862: "The war must go on; and we must carry it on, on a scale commensurate with the importance of the interests at stake. . . . The war was forced upon us, and we must conquer."

In February came news of the sailing of the second stone fleet, consisting of old wooden vessels loaded with stones that would be used to block the channel of Charleston Harbor.

Lieutenant George N. Macy of the 20th Massachusetts received a box of gifts from the town to be distributed to his men, who in turn had sent several hundred dollars home, saved from their pay and allowances, for their families and friends. Even the meager pay of the servicemen was welcomed by the impoverished families at Nantucket.

The *Mirror* printed the news from Washington that President Lincoln had received from the Emperor of Siam several gifts: a solid gold sword, two perfect elephant's tusks, and a daguerreotype of the Emperor with his son sitting on his knee. (It was on that occasion that the Emperor also offered President Lincoln a gift of elephants to help him win the war.)

In April, the *Mirror* wrote at length on "The Crime of Secession," describing how the actions of the southern leaders had threatened the destruction of a happy and prosperous Union. It was claimed that the situation arose when "From the germs planted at Plymouth and Jamestown sprang two distinct peoples. . . . The colony at Plymouth was founded upon religious and moral principles. That at Jamestown for the gain of gold. . . . That incongruity has disorganized the Union."

In the spring of 1862, the news was almost totally taken up with reports that General George B. McClellan, moving after a winter of inactivity to commence the Peninsula Campaign, was headed for Richmond. The Army of the Potomac and the men of Nantucket had great faith in McClellan, and the news of his expected victories was awaited by the local population.

How Nantucket received its news was pictured by the *Mirror* on May 31:

Just after noon on Thursday last, the schooner Susan from New Bedford was seen approaching from the westward, with a signal flying that she had news of importance . . . as she neared Brant Point an eager crowd collected on the Straight Wharf to learn the tidings. Conspicuous on the wharf was "General Clark" (Town Crier Billy Clark), dressed in a brand new uniform, with two small ensigns flying in his cap, the most impatient person in the crowd. When she arrived at the wharf, a paper was thrown on shore, and the news of the battle of Hanover Court House was read to the excited multitude. An extra was immediately issued from our office, and soon the rich, musical voice of the General was heard in the street, crying "Eere's your Mirror extra: only two cents; Great Battle near Richmond." The extras sold like hot cakes, and the General, with his pockets filled with pennies, went home that night as rich as a lord.

July brought the grim results of McClellan's campaign: the death of Jared Hunter at Turkey Bend, the death of Charles D. Barnard before Richmond, and the wounding of E. G. W. Cartwright and Corporal John Summerhayes. On July 4, 1862, the losses in the Peninsula brought President Lincoln's first draft call for 300,000 volunteers to serve three years or until the war ended.

A town meeting was convened in the Atheneum. Patriotic speeches pleaded for more manpower to reinforce the army, in view of the newly recognized strength of the Confederate forces, and the town voted unanimously to offer a bounty of $100 per man. It was emphasized that, as the national draft loomed, the bounty applied only to volunteers. A Nantucket man who enlisted in 1862 was entitled to $100 from the town, $100 from the U.S., $12 per month for family allowance and $13 per month for pay, making a total of $500 for the year, "which will probably be the time required, and will be a very good compensation." The town appointed Frank J. Crosby and William Summerhayes as recruiting agents.

On July 4, Frederick W. Mitchell, aide to General McClellan, wrote from "Not Quite as near as Richmond":

On this beautiful morn of the 4th the bands and bugles . . . make the woods in which perhaps 20,000 of us are encamped re-echo; we who are left will give thanks. . . . You do not know how we worship our leader! Napoleon never had the confidence of his troops more than McClellan . . . do you wonder we love him! . . . All our moves, whether falling back or advancing, have been a complete success, and though it is horrible, the slaughter of the enemy has been three or four to our one.

The confidence in McClellan stemmed from his concern for his men and his reputation for fighting against great odds, albeit the odds were usually conjured by his own fantastic overestimations of enemy strength. He was constantly calling for more troops. Now, after the losses on the road to Richmond, a new tone of apprehension appeared in the press:

> The rebels are everywhere active and confident. McClellan's army is barely out of danger, although seventeen miles from the rebel capital. Halleck's army has been divided and the larger portion of it is threatened by two rebel columns. . . . Washington itself is seriously threatened.

In July, the pressure and sadness of the war was being felt increasingly on the island. Two young men, William F. Barnard and Edward P. Chase, returned home, discharged for disability after the Peninsula Campaign. Barnard reported that the 22nd Massachusetts Regiment had 400 men left from an original 1100 volunteers. Chase served with the 10th New York Regiment, but was too feeble to take part in the battles. The Sanitary Commission pleaded for more supplies to comfort the troops, and William Summerhayes, father of John Summerhayes, sent two boxes of articles to the Nantucket boys in the 20th Massachusetts.

In August, a new contingent of volunteers departed Nantucket on the steamer. They were all young lads, including nineteen-year-old Josiah Fitch Murphey, who jumped on board as buoyantly as if going on a vacation. As the *Mirror* saw it:

> Their clean and boyish faces were lit up with smiles and their light and gay converse had no shadow upon it of the future. Very different was the feelings of their fathers who shook them by the hand and attempted to bid them goodbye but found the expression to die in their throats. . . . May they come back again for those to lean on who have so nobly given them to their broken and bleeding country.

Nantucket continued to present a dismal appearance, especially on its once prosperous waterfront.

"We almost cry out, where are the ships?" a local editorialist anguished:

> Only one now lies at our wharves. . . . the Narragansett, one of the best of the fleet, has lain at the Straight Wharf since the summer of 1860. The wharves, except the Straight, are dropping away piecemeal. When shall these thoroughfares and neglected wharves assume the cheerful look of twenty years ago?

The Nantucket men of 1861 were eager to volunteer for both the army and the navy. They were impelled to sign up by the patriotic atmosphere prevailing in the Commonwealth and by editorials in their local newspapers. However, by 1862, that spirit began to wane. That summer, the Nantucket *Mirror* seemed to throw down the glove to the fainthearted: Writing from Harrison's Landing, Virginia, where the 20th Massachusetts was encamped with McClellan's army, a correspondent signed "S," who was none other than John Summerhayes, wrote to inspire the local recruiting effort:

> Now, where are the descendents from that old stock which has made Nantucket's name so well known, the world over? Has the blood run out? Is there not enough patriotic feeling in Nantucket to raise forty men without drafting? . . . I would rather die a thousand deaths than living, know that our glorious Union, bought with the the blood of our forefathers, should be torn asunder by these miserable Southern hounds. . . . Where is the old Nantucket pluck! Show it boldly now, if ever. Step up and enlist! . . . Come and join us; our ranks are not full. Company I still has room for as many Nantucket boys as will come undrafted; if you allow yourselves to be drafted, for Heaven's sake join some new regiment!

Recruiting was spurred by the announcement of an impending draft call. As the war went on, the early enthusiasm to enlist in a short and glorious war had faded, and the stern realities of the casualty lists and disabled soldiers made their impression. In August, there was an appeal for men to fill up the 32nd Massachusetts, a reminder that "Drafted Men Get No Bounty," and a special appeal for local men to join the new ironclad Navy: "Let every Jack-tar take a fresh quid and final hitch to his trowsers, and then go in for glory, prize money and the constitution." The paper published the names of nineteen volunteers, and it was announced that Nantucket had met its quota under the second call, issued in August, for 300,000 volunteers to serve nine months.

That same month, another town meeting voted to pay $100 bonuses to men who enlisted for the nine months. Patriotic speeches by Reverend Bodfish of the Methodist Church and Reverend Hosmer of the Congregational Church resulted in a unanimous vote, partly inspired by aversion to the draft, to raise taxes to pay the new bounty.

A writer from Boston described the arrival of the Nantucket volunteers in the city, the tents on the Common reminding them of the annual sheep-shearing holidays, and where, in front of the Old South Church, each new recruit was announced by the ringing of a bell captured by General Benjamin Butler in New Orleans.

In Nantucket, the state of the economy was apparent from the news that William Patterson was moving his house from Water Street to be rebuilt in Chatham, at a cost of $400, "which expense is incurred since he cannot sell the house and land at this time."

The *Inquirer* published the August letter of President Lincoln to Horace Greeley in which he stated his war aims, emphasizing the preservation of the Union over the issue of slavery. This, claimed the paper, "takes the ground the *Inquirer* has always taken. . . . We have always insisted the business of the nation was with the rebellion. That to crush these traitors to the earth was the only duty of the Government."

The paper also reported the enlistment of all the three-year volunteers and sixteen nine-months men. It then published the honor roll, showing enlistments of 160 men in the army and 90 in the navy, as of August 1862.

In the last days of August, the Confederate Army inflicted a major defeat on the Union Army at the Second Battle of Bull Run, resulting in over 15,000 Union casualties. News of the tragedy reached Nantucket on September 1, and was followed by a large gathering in the Atheneum to arrange for contributions to relieve the suffering soldiers. School children were enlisted to pick and scrape lint, and young girls who could sew made bandages. Local artists arranged for a musical concert to benefit the cause of soldiers' relief. At the end of the week, an assortment of goods including clothing, pillows, blankets, food, and lint, sufficient to fill fifteen cartons, was sent to the U.S. Sanitary Commission in Boston, along with $500 in cash that had been raised for the cause.

The town honored the nine-months volunteers at a gathering in Hussey's Hall that featured a dinner for 100 people, followed by speeches from local dignitaries. The party then adjourned to Pantheon Hall for music and dancing. It was noted with approval that nothing stronger than coffee was served.

In September, the town learned of Leander F. Alley's promotion to the rank of second lieutenant, for bravery in action before Richmond. Nantucket members of Company I of the 20th Massachusetts made up a purse to purchase a sword for the popular leader, a testimonial of respect from his companions in arms. The money was sent to a Nantucket merchant to purchase the sword and send it to the new officer.

The battle of Antietam, fought on September 17, 1862, was reported in dispatches from General McClellan as a complete victory, with the rebel army making for the Potomac River in a perfect panic and the general following as fast as his men could move. Rumors of the great battle mentioned heavy casualties on both sides and reported that General James Longstreet had been wounded and taken prisoner, which was false.

In September, the Boston *Journal* reported the arrival of fifty-four volunteers from Nantucket accompanied by Frank Crosby, the recruiting officer and a selectman of the town. Fifty-two men had already volunteered for three years, and they were as fine a body of men as ever seen in Boston. "No one can doubt the patriotism of the good people of Nantucket," the reporter noted.

Writing from Readville, the correspondent of the 45th Massachusetts sent a picture of camp life in the new regiment. After the Cape Cod boys of Company D raised a company flag decorated with a codfish as their emblem, the Nantucketers and Vineyard boys of Company H responded by raising a banner showing a whale impaled upon a harpoon to inspire the island troops. Noting that "the codfish and segars arrived safe," and that new uniforms had been provided the men, it was reported that the regiment was soon to be ordered to North Carolina.

In November of 1862, Massachusetts held a gubernatorial election with General Charles Devens, Jr., running against Governor John A. Andrew. The *Inquirer* editorialized in support of the Democratic, or People's, ticket, principally to defeat the reelection of Senator Charles Sumner and his stand for abolition." The People's Party say first put down the rebels and then look out for the Negro." The Republicans won handily.

In November, Private Benjamin F. Burdick was sent to New Bern, North Carolina, where he joined the 45th Massachusetts and other regiments on a drive toward Whitehall, Kinston, and Goldsboro. The Union forces destroyed thirty-six miles of railroad and captured hundreds of prisoners.

An anecdote reported in the Nantucket *Journal* offers humorous evidence of the "culture shock" experienced by some New England boys when faced with the social realities of some impoverished southern whites.

Burdick was driving an ambulance wagon, heading back to New Bern, and while traveling through a dark mountain ravine spied a little log hut. Seeking to find a hearty meal, he drove up to the cabin and "an old woman with a face like a pig's" came out and shouted,

"Where did you come from and what are you doing here?"

He said he was coming from Goldsboro and wanted something to eat. Then he asked her if there were any "Secesh" round there.

"Why, gracious, what's them?" she asked.

He asked, "Are you and your folks for the Union?"

"Why sartin!" she said, "here comes my old man now."

Just at that moment there came a gaunt-eyed, slim-livered, cadaverous, yellow-skinned North Carolinean.

"Look heah," said the woman, "this sojer wants to know if you be for the Union?"

The old fellow looked more astonished than the woman. I asked the old man what he thought of the war.

"What war!" he exclaimed. "You mean the Revolution?"

I said, "We call it the Rebellion."

"Ah, why," he brightened up, "We gave those Britishers fits, didn't we?"

DECEMBER OF 1862 WAS TO PROVE the most tragic month in Nantucket history. As the 20th Massachusetts camped at Falmouth, Virginia, awaiting orders to cross the Rappahannock River, the Boston *Herald* tallied the regiment's losses to date. The casualties were appalling. The 20th had lost 398 men at Ball's Bluff, 145 on the Peninsula, and 147 at Antietam. Of the original regiment, which left Massachusetts in September 1861, there were now only 145 survivors. All the senior officers had been wounded or disabled and the regiment was now under strength, with fewer than 400 men led by Acting Major George N. Macy, of Nantucket. In December, twenty-five Massachusetts regiments were at Fredericksburg, Virginia, and eleven at New Bern, North Carolina, with large contingents of Nantucketers at both places.

With the news delayed for a week, the *Mirror* of December 20 finally published the grim report from Fredericksburg: five Nantucketers killed (a number later raised to eight) and thirteen wounded. According to custom, when the thrice-weekly steamer from the mainland arrived with sad tidings, its flag would be at half-mast, alerting those on shore to the tragic news. When the steamer arrived with those first casualty reports, the scene on the wharf, with anxious relatives awaiting word of loved ones at the front, became pathetic. The crowd was weeping before the steamer docked.

Among the mourned was Lieutenant Leander F. Alley, whose body was brought home on Christmas Day by the wounded Josiah F. Murphey, for the first military funeral on Nantucket. Schools and businesses closed and the entire town turned out for what was to become the first of many burials in the "Soldiers' Graves" at Prospect Hill Cemetery.

Ironically, as Confederate General Robert E. Lee's men were shooting down Union soldiers at Fredericksburg, Federal troops in North Carolina were on the march in the Goldsboro Expedition, a nine-day excursion into the interior of the state intended to prevent the

Confederates from retaking the eastern areas of the state, which were held by Union forces. Several days after that disaster, Union forces, including the 45th Massachusetts, which like the 20th Massachusetts had one company of Nantucketers, met the rebels in a series of three principal battles—Kinston, Whitehall, and Goldsboro. The casualties included two Nantucket men dead and eight wounded. Although the Goldsboro Expedition might be counted a minor Union victory, the loss of yet more island boys added to the desperate gloom of the island as the year drew to a close.

Thus ended the year 1862. A year that had started with a spirit of patriotism and determination ended in the saddest of Christmas seasons, with many Nantucket men dead or wounded and the funeral of Leander Alley occupying the minds and hearts of the town. Nantucket was deep in despair, and the end of the war was nowhere in sight.

1863

THE PIVOTAL YEAR OF THE WAR dawned on a Nantucket mourning its lost sons from Fredericksburg and the Goldsboro Expedition. With ten men killed in action the previous month, the island brooded about the future. Sadness pervaded the new year. A poignant letter to the *Mirror* from Lieutenant Benjamin F. Weeks, quartermaster of the 28th Massachusetts, told of the death of one Nantucketer, Lieutenant Clinton Swain, killed at Fredericksburg with the 81st Pennsylvania. He was shot thirty minutes after remarking, "If I live to come out of this fight, I shall tell Ben how lucky he is to get clear of all this hard fighting." When he heard the news of Swain's death, his colonel cried, "Poor little Clint is gone! My God, how awful! I will give any man a hundred dollars that will recover his body."

The most touching of all letters was that to Sarah Mitchell, mother of Leander F. Alley, written from Falmouth, Virginia, on December 29 and signed by George N. Macy, Henry L. Abbott, Oliver W. Holmes, Jr., and all the surviving officers of the 20th Massachusetts, who "desire to express to you their sympathy in the terrible loss you have sustained. There was no man in the regiment superior to Lieut. Alley in honesty, energy and decision of character. In battle he was wonderfully cool, collected and clear-headed. . . . He was unquestionably an invaluable officer."

The reorganized Soldiers' Relief Society reported on the activities of its sixty-two members; they had prepared bundles of clothing, foodstuffs, and other creature comforts to be shipped to the Sanitary Commission and thence directly to Nantucket soldiers. Clothing and blankets were most appreciated, they reported, but they also sent soap, bandages, and a little medicinal wine and brandy.

A single paragraph in the *Mirror* noted President Lincoln's Emancipation Proclamation, which stated that as of January 1, 1863, all persons held as slaves in the disloyal states would be and henceforward shall be forever free. The declaration by the President was a war measure, an act of justice, warranted by the Constitution upon military necessity.

A Nantucketer who signed himself "Forty-fifth" (Corporal William Hussey Macy) was wounded at Kinston, and wrote to the papers about other Nantucket men serving in North Carolina with the 45th Massachusetts. He wrote that he was "laboring under a severe attack of rifle-ball and army surgeon. The 45th has received its 'baptism of fire'; said baptism being no sprinkling either but a liberal immersion." He delivered a lively description of the battle of Kinston, which took place on December 14, almost simultaneously with the battle of Fredericksburg: "In both cases, Nantucket boys held posts of honor in the front, and the flag was never disgraced in their hands."

The same correspondent reported a week later that he and the other wounded Nantucket boys, Obed Coffin, Davis Hall, and Frank Turner, were doing well. The Nantucket men rejoiced that the enemy at Kinston had been commanded by the same General Nathaniel Evans who had fought the Nantucket boys at Ball's Bluff in 1861.

Another Nantucketer wrote from the army hospital in Philadelphia with praise for the brave 20th Massachusetts, which "has won for itself a niche and a name in history," and remembered hours spent with his boyhood friends, Clint Swain and Leander Alley.

In February, the *Mirror* wrote an editorial praising "The Colored Regiments," and encouraging the enlistment of more free blacks in the Union Army:

> This war is in fact a war between the defenders of slavery and the advocates of freedom. . . . The proclamation of the President has nominally made millions of freemen. But that Proclamation must be published at the point of the bayonet. . . . Who, then, are more clearly indicated as messengers of freedom than the colored freemen of the whole country, the escaped slaves of the South.

The *Inquirer* of February 18, in a strong editorial deploring the dismal prospects of the war, lashed out at "The Abolitionists," who had brought on the war and divided the country, and predicted the country would be better off to end the war and let the South go its own way:

> If the North hangs together, time will give us the victory. The natural increase of the Northern States will soon make them overshadow the South. . . . We find the South but little above the Indians. . . . When they have got their Confederacy established let them remain in it, and . . . never more trust another one of the treacherous and arrogant brood.

The next issue announced that Alfred Macy, Esquire, had assumed editorial control of the *Inquirer* and would devote its columns to the support of Abraham Lincoln and his policy. Not coincidentally, the *Inquirer* would run no more anti-abolitionist editorials.

John W. Summerhayes published a lengthy letter to the "Ladies of Nantucket," in which he claimed that very little of the aid from the Sanitary Commission reached the troops, and the real need was for a Soldiers' Relief Society to provide aid for the families of the dead and wounded. He mentioned that Captain Henry L. Abbott had written to the selectmen with a similar concern for the families of his Nantucket men. The emphasis of the society should be upon aid for local families in need, and the ladies were to carry it forward.

Amid news of a new draft of all men between the ages of 35 and 45, a list was published of Nantucket men who were exempted from service for reasons ranging from "imbecility" to "only son of widow."

Inducements to enlist in the Heavy Artillery Corps for defense of the New England Coast were reassuring: "The men shall not be called away from this vicinity. . . . There are no long marches, no heavy knapsacks, and food, clothing and attendance are abundant."

During the winter, the Sons and Daughters of Nantucket resident in San Francisco, mostly former islanders who had left the island when the whaling declined, gathered for a meeting at the U.S. Courthouse in that city. Their purpose was to raise money to aid the families of Nantucket men who had lost their lives in the war. Their island home was still close to the hearts of those enjoying "uninterrupted prosperity" in San Francisco, and was manifest in their raising $674.94, which they sent to aid needy Nantucket families.

From New Bern, North Carolina, "Forty-Fifth" wrote to say the Nantucket boys were in good shape, despite a trip south on a ship filled with cattle and drovers. "I would commend to all travellers of quiet, refined habits, the delights of a steerage passage in a transport, in the agreeable companionship of canalmen, beeves and bullock-drivers." He noted that news from the war reached home every other day in Nantucket, but the news from home took a week or ten days to reach the front.

The *Inquirer* continued its squabble with the *Mirror* by calling it the champion of the Democratic Party in its constant criticism of the President and his policies.

The April 22 edition of the *Inquirer* urged a policy of patience upon the public and wrote of the bright prospects for the Union armies. On the eve of the battle of Chancellorsville, the paper's editorial encouraged faith in Massachusetts' own General Joseph Hooker: "Hooker has, unquestionably, the best army ever collected on this continent. He is a careful fighting man. He is resolved upon dealing a crushing blow."

In an editorial entitled "The Arming of the Negroes," the *Inquirer* supported the idea of raising black troops:

Although the public had been divided on the question of arming slaves in the early years, now, after the loss of a hundred thousand men, the participation of black men in uniform would be invaluable. It was said that the black man in the South was perfectly acclimated, inured to labor, acquainted with the roads, and longing to render assistance.

Most important, his only hope of freedom is the success of the national government: "He has been a slave; he will not become a slave again."

The success of Admiral David Porter and his fleet on the Mississippi, closing in on the fortress of Vicksburg, was acclaimed as a great naval victory. It also allowed Admiral David Farragut to operate with the northern forces up and down river from the enemy remaining, and ensured that the rebels must either leave Vicksburg or starve.

The encouraging news from the war fronts provided the incentive for the island to plan a Fourth of July celebration. Beginning in June, meetings were held in the Atheneum Hall to plan a festive occasion at the Agricultural Fair Grounds. The affair was intended to garner public support for the Soldiers' Relief Society, provide entertainment for the young people of the island, and offer a display of local patriotism.

While awaiting the Fourth of July, Nantucket read of the long siege of Vicksburg, the uncertain fate of Grant's campaign, and the dreaded news that General Lee had begun his long-expected invasion of Pennsylvania. The armies were on the move, and the town anxiously awaited each day's news.

On June 27, the *Mirror*, with some anxiety, wrote: "Where will Lee turn up? There is great uncertainty as to Lee's whereabouts. Portions of his force have made their appearance in Pennsylvania and Maryland. Chambersburg, Pa., is in their possession, and the whole border is in a state of trepidation."

At the same time, Nantucket was preoccupied with the impending return of the Nantucket men serving with the 45th Regiment in North Carolina. Company H was composed almost entirely of Nantucket men, and the terms of the nine-month enlistees was expiring. They had fought at Kinston, Weldon, and Goldsboro, losing from the original fifty-four Nantucketers two men in battle and three who died of disease. A meeting was held at the Atheneum to arrange for a proper reception upon their arrival in Nantucket. The veterans, however, declined the offer of a public reception, pleading the ill health of some and the desire of all to see their families at once on arriving home. Veteran correspondent William H. Macy wrote that the men would respectfully decline anything like a public reception or ovation, and their wishes were respected.

Nantucket's Fourth of July celebration was a great success, although the island did not yet have the news of the Union victories at Gettysburg and Vicksburg. Hundreds gathered at the Agricultural Grounds to enjoy the food and pageantry, but fireworks and cigars were forbidden. The bands played patriotic music as a large wagon, drawn by four horses, appeared carrying thirty-five prettily dressed young ladies, each bearing the name of one of the states loyal to the Union. Miss Mary Nelson, dressed as West Virginia, was greeted with "We welcome thee, Western Virginia," and recited a poem written by Lucy Starbuck.

Not until July 11 did the *Inquirer* and the *Mirror* have the chance to write of "The Glorious News." The island was thrilled by the news of Lee's defeat and Grant's capture of Vicksburg, both coming on the Fourth of July weekend. When the news first reached the island, the bells were rung, the public halls illuminated, and preparations were made for a fireworks display, which was canceled by a heavy fog. The display did come off the following evening, when Main Street was filled with people and the fireworks showed to great advantage. Rumors of peace proposals filled the air, and many thought the war was almost over.

Nantucket men of the 20th Massachusetts had been in the front line facing Pickett's Charge at Gettysburg. Lieutenant Colonel George N. Macy had his left hand amputated because of a gunshot wound, Private Henry Jones was killed, and six other local men were wounded. [For an account of the 20th Massachusetts in action at Gettysburg, see Appendix, p. 49.]

The heavy Union losses at Gettysburg prompted the next draft call for the middle of July, which provoked riots in New York City and Boston. In Nantucket, 117 men were called, of which seventy-eight were required to serve, but great confusion resulted when it was found that many men had left Nantucket for California and whaling voyages, while others were already in the service. Bonuses were available for those who enlisted, none for those who were drafted. The

New York riots were blamed on the excesses of the Democratic Party in that city, which claimed the draft unfairly burdened the poor, since it allowed exemption to the wealthy, who could either hire substitutes or pay a fee of $300.

Nantucket soon heard a humorous complaint from one of its colorful sons, Elisha P. Gardner, who described himself as "A Drafted Volunteer." Writing from Fort Independence in Boston Harbor, he described his surprise on reading that he had been drafted in Nantucket. On July 15, 1862, he had enlisted in the 39th Massachusetts and was discharged the next March. Then, on April 13, 1863, he enlisted in the 14th Massachusetts Heavy Artillery and was sent to one of the forts that guarded Boston Harbor. Then he found himself drafted in July.

"Not having enough men on the island to fill her quota," he wrote, "the patriotic island of Nantucket has adopted a method of her own, namely, drafting her volunteers that are now in the army, thereby reviving the old saying: 'Get money, get it it honestly if you can, but get it.' He figured he was now entitled to two bounties, one from Boston where he enlisted, and one from Nantucket where he was drafted (a new act of Congress having approved the bonus for draftees). "I shall always remember I was a drafted volunteer, and received two bounties, and yet it was done legally."

Gardner did return home to collect his bounty in August, and wrote to thank Nantucket for making him a drafted volunteer. "Think you Nantucket will be forgotten in this crisis of the world's history? Long will she be remembered by me, as I go away to count over my different bounties. . . . Nantucket is not so bad a place after all, and that there really is Polity in War." The island had not heard the last of Elisha P. Gardner.

He never left Nantucket. He stayed on to become the island's new recruiting officer, with headquarters in the Hussey Block on Main Street. In August, he wrote to Nantucket's young men, "Fall In Double Quick." This was their chance to enroll in the 2nd Regiment of Heavy Artillery, where they would receive $450 bounty and $13 per month, rations, and clothes. "There is a long dreary winter fast approach-

ing, and what is there on Nantucket for a young man to do this coming winter? This regiment is being raised for garrison duty in New
Bern, North Carolina, where there is no marching to be done. Let us
raise a brave crew and go to North Carolina, and man the yards, and
take the helm, and pilot her back into the Union, and keep her there.
. . . Now is the day of salvation. . . . Fall in for roll call."

He followed with the news that the 1st Regiment was full, and the
last company would go with the 2nd Regiment—the last regiment of
Heavy Artillery to be raised in Massachusetts. "You well know the long
marches belonging to the infantry, and the fatigues and exposures of
cavalry. You all know that in Heavy Artillery you avoid all this. . . . If
you wish to go under a Nantucket officer, one of your old schoolmates,
and a drafted volunteer, enlist without delay in this 2nd regiment of
Heavy Artillery, Colonel Frankle. Delays are dangerous. Hurry up, or
the regiment will be full, and then look out for the second draft."

A meeting of abolitionists that had been called for the evening of
Sunday, September 6, 1863, at the Atheneum was postponed to Monday, September 7, and moved to the Methodist Church, as being "more
commodious." The meeting was led by Nathaniel Barney, and features
of the discussion were the barbarism of slavery; the massacre at
Lawrence, Kansas,* and the terrible consequences of the war that
were attributed to slavery. The principal speaker was Aaron M. Pow-
ell, whose Nantucket forebears had sought support for the abolitionist
cause. Nathaniel Barney, one of Nantucket's most prominent abolitionists, recounted the history of slavery in the nation and spoke of
the many attempts at compromise that had led from one concession
to another and, finally, to civil war. He extolled the great victory of
President Lincoln's Proclamation of Emancipation, and he rejoiced
that church and state were joined in the progress toward freedom.

Lieutenant Leander F. Alley was poignantly remembered when it

---

*Lawrence, Kansas, a bastion of Yankee abolitionists, had been attacked by proslavery forces in 1856 and became
the target of the Confederate guerrilla leader William Clarke Quantrill. His band of 450 men conducted a
vicious raid on August 21, 1863, killing 182 men and boys and burning 185 buildings. The U. S. Cavalry pur-
sued the outlaws through three states, shooting or hanging many of them. Quantrill was not captured until May
1865, when he was killed near Taylorsville, Kentucky.

was learned that the elegant sword purchased for him by his comrades of the 20th Massachusetts had been located and would be returned to Nantucket. Lieutenant Alley had died at Fredericksburg before the sword could be delivered to him, "owing to the negligence of the agent of the Express Company," the paper noted. "The sword was found at Hagerstown, Maryland, and has been restored to the custody of Lt. Alley's mother." The sword is now in the collection of the Nantucket Historical Association.

The Soldiers' Relief Society reported the dispatch of fifteen boxes of clothing and necessities for the troops, including shirts, socks, pillows, sheets, caps, and mittens sent to the Sanitary Commission. It also announced the receipt of $145.00 from Captain Abbott's company of the 20th Massachusetts to be used for the soldiers and their families in Nantucket.

November 4 brought news of the Republican triumph in the state election, with Governor John A. Andrew winning 412 votes in Nantucket compared with Democrat Henry W. Paine's total of forty-one. All other Republicans won the town by identical votes. The *Inquirer* wrote: "Thank God for success. It is a triumph of liberty over despotism, of principle over passion."

In December, the town was worried again about the draft, for of the fifty-eight men demanded of Nantucket, only eleven had volunteered, and the remainder would have to be drafted. A plea in the *Mirror* urged the men of Nantucket that were still eligible to volunteer, for which they would receive $2.69 a day, more than they could earn in Nantucket in the winter. Those who could not go were urged to find men who would.

The selectmen held a town meeting in December 1863, and were authorized to make loans of $300 each to needy families of volunteers, to be repaid from the volunteers' bonuses. Another expenditure of $2000 was made for the care of sick and wounded soldiers. The measures were taken to persuade more men to volunteer, and to assure the Nantucket men at home and abroad that the town was acting on their behalf.

The year ended with a vote at town meeting to care for the sick and wounded and to lend every assistance to the war effort. The despair that marked the year's beginning had yielded to a determination to weather through, despite the cost. Regardless of the pain and weariness it brought, the war must go on until the rebels were defeated, and Nantucketers would see it to the end.

Nantucketers could not know that 1864 would bring more than their share of tragedy.

1864

THE PROSPECT FOR NANTUCKET as the year 1864 dawned was hopeful, and cautious optimism had replaced the gloom of early 1863. Recognizing that the country had endured three years of a devastating war, and that although the North had made many mistakes it was now proving its power and dedication, the community felt a renewed hope and determination. The great northern victories of Gettysburg, Vicksburg, and Chattanooga were proof that the tide had turned and that the Union Army would soon roll over the enemy with an irresistible force.

The recruitment of Nantucket men continued, recruiting officer Frank Crosby reporting thirty-nine more enlistments, including several veterans who had come home and reenlisted. One of them was Alexander E. Ray, aged 18, who had served two years with the 42nd Ohio Volunteers under General Don Carlos Buell and under General Ulysses S. Grant at Vicksburg, and had then returned to Nantucket and signed up for two more years.

An unusual incident at the Readville training camp, near Dedham, interrupted the pace of Nantucket recruiting. Surgeon A. A. Stocker, upon examining the Nantucket boys, rejected four of the volunteers on the grounds that they were "under 16 years of age," and turned them away from the army camp with no means of returning home. One lad admitted to being under age, but the others claimed they were of age and produced letters from their mothers stating they were over eighteen. Alexander E. Ray, the 18-year old veteran, was also rejected for "weak lungs," without being examined by the doctor.

The most shocking treatment was afforded one lad who stated he was "almost nineteen." The surgeon asked him how he knew, and he replied, "My mother told me." The doctor then asked, "How in the devil does your mother know?" This abuse of the recruit and slander of his mother provoked a flood of criticism and a drought of recruits from Nantucket.

Meanwhile, President Lincoln called for 200,000 more men to fill the Union ranks, and a spirited meeting of citizens was held at the Atheneum to promote the enlistment of Nantucket's quota of forty-seven more men. Reverend Karcher of the Unitarian Church gave a speech indicating his belief that the war would not long continue, and that privates were now being paid more than officers, and fared better on a march, in addition to running infinitely less risk in battle. As a final inducement for forty-six men to enlist, he offered to fill the last enlistment himself. As the minister had already served as an army chaplain, his opinions and enthusiasm were warmly received.

One speaker made the mistake of provoking Nantucket women when he remarked, "I understand that the women of Nantucket influence the men against enlisting." This inspired a response in the *Mirror* from a woman who spoke as "one who has done all she could," pleading for higher motives and more cheerful cooperation on the part of the mothers, wives, and sisters of Nantucket. She urged the women not to retard the great cause by useless tears or entreaties, but to encourage their husbands and sons to go forth to defend the government and bring peace.

A letter dated January 25, 1864, gave a colorful description of a Nantucketer's view of wartime Washington. Writing as "Conscript, Co. C, Provost Guard," he reported on a trip to Washington in a unit of five sergeants that was guarding a detail of newly drafted conscripts. Starting out from Boston, they traveled to New York and then to Jersey City, where they departed with 367 "big-bounty men" in box cars, moving "like a turkey wading through tar." They stopped

for welcome meals in Philadelphia and Baltimore, where they board-
ed "real passenger cars" to Washington. There they stayed at the
"Soldiers' Rest," a huge bunkhouse, 300 feet long with seven stoves
down the center. The food at the Soldiers' Rest was not easily forgotten: raw ham and bread for breakfast, bread and ham for dinner,
and ham and bread for supper. After delivering the troops to Alexandria on flat cars "going like lightening," the work of the provost guard
was done. They returned to the Rest, to find themselves under guard
till morning, when they were given passes to stroll around Washington until eight at night. Washington was then under tight military
control, and "I had to have a pass with my Captain's name attached
and, like a big boy, be in at eight or be punished." Two of them did
have their papers extended so they could go to the theater and see
"Camille, or the Fate of the Coquette," which was enjoyed, but the
overwhelming picture of Washington was dull and dreary. "If I was
after pleasure, I should not go to Washington," he remarked.

The Nantucket correspondent returned to Boston in twenty-eight
hours, a much shorter journey than the outgoing trip. On their arrival,
the general made a speech, saying they had done what no other provost
guard unit had done: landed all the recruits and returned with the
unit intact. He was glad to have a group of men he could trust.

In February, the young men of Nantucket held a "War Meeting" at
the Atheneum Hall with the object of promoting more enlistments.
Called to order by returned veteran William H. Wood, the meeting
elected Arthur E. Jenks as secretary and nineteen vice-presidents. Reverend Hosmer delivered a patriotic speech, telling the audience that
a blue coat was a badge of honor, and that it would be more honored
when the cruel war was over and one could say, "I was in that great
army who fought to crush a wicked rebellion." Reverend Stetson rose
to add a tribute to the woman who was asked if she were willing for
her husband to go to war: "Willing? Yes! And if I had been a man, I
would have gone myself long ago!" Reverend Karcher endorsed the
words of the preceding speakers, spoke of his thrill when seeing the
American flag after traveling in distant lands, and then offered three

cheers for Colonel George N. Macy and the boys of Nantucket.

Alfred Macy, Esquire, called for a speech from young Alexander C. Ray, recently returned from two years' service under General Grant; he gave a vivid description of the war.

William H. Wood rose to the call of the crowd. He had first enlisted in response to Lincoln's first call for 75,000 volunteers, in 1861, joining the 3rd Battalion Rifles of Massachusetts Volunteers. After being home six months, he reenlisted in Company D, 25th Massachusetts Volunteers, where he served under General Ambrose Burnside in North Carolina. He was discharged for wounds received in battle, returned home for a year, then reenlisted in the 56th Massachusetts Volunteers. Nantucket was his home and he was proud to hail from it. He said the only way to conquer the rebels was with cold steel and musket balls.

Alfred Macy proposed raising a "Citizen's Bounty Fund" to stimulate enlistments, and started the fund by contributing $50 from his pocket, which was appreciated by the meeting. John W. Barrett, president of the Pacific National Bank, followed with a pledge of $200, "a very liberal contribution." A committee of three men was formed to collect the funds, and the meeting adjourned to meet again on Thursday, three nights later.

At the next meeting, the committee reported collecting a sum of $360, plus the receipt of $50 from two young ladies, Miss Lydia Bunker and Miss Harriet P. Winn, for a total of $410. William Wood rose to suggest that the funds be disbursed by the committee of three, and not given to the Sanitary Commission, as he had no faith in it. During seven months in the hospital, he had received nothing from the commission.

Reverend Karcher rose to corroborate William Wood's tale, saying that after the battle of Fredericksburg he had visited a division hospital and found many sick men needing care who were fed only boiled rice and black coffee and had not seen a chaplain for weeks. At a nearby office of the Sanitary Commission he was told the men could receive no extra items without a certificate from the surgeon stating they were entitled to some luxury. The surgeons did not care, and the attendants often intercepted things meant for the sick and wounded. The Nantucket people could take better care of their own boys.

The news also arrived that Miss Anna Gardner, who had taught for several years in Nantucket, had accepted a post as teacher in the new Freedmen's School in New Bern, North Carolina. From her early years, Miss Gardner had been in the forefront of the abolitionist movement, and her decision to go south to help the former slave children was inspired by her choosing to go "where she feels there is more need for her services in a cause she has long held an interest."

More news from North Carolina came in correspondence from Morehead City dated February 14, when a Nantucket sergeant (possibly none other than Elisha P. Gardner) wrote: "So let the glorious stars and stripes defiantly fly over Morehead City; they can proudly defy, and the troops that are here can bravely repulse any rebel force that may attack."

The sergeant added, no doubt with an eye on prospective recruits from the hometown:

> If some of the young men that are walking around home doing nothing would only enlist and come out here and help us, we could sweep this State of every rebel. . . . For all a soldier's life is said by some to be a hard life, yet after all, there is some glory in fighting for the glorious stars and stripes. I never enjoyed myself better, than since I have been in the army, and if the young men of Nantucket will enlist and come out here in North Carolina, I will see that they enjoy themselves. I am perfectly willing to remain in the army until this rebellion is put down. I wouldn't take my discharge if it was offered to me. We have a very good General (General Butler) in command of us, and this is a very good department; all we want is a few more troops, and we will drive the rebels to the wall...We have plenty to eat out here, good quarters, plenty of clothing and what is better, we get our pay every two months. We are in good fighting order and will give a good account of ourselves, and keep the stars and stripes waving.

March brought the call of President Lincoln for 500,000 more men to fill the Union ranks for the final year of the war. Nantucket had a quota of 100 men, but had already furnished 163, so had a surplus of sixty-three for future calls. On March 12, the *Mirror* published this information:

Number enlisted here 51; number enlisted abroad 5;

Drafted in July and entered service 3;

Drafted in July and commuted 7;

Drafted in July and furnished substitute 4;

Reenlisted 10;

Men in Navy 83

Total 163

For the first time, the *Mirror* referred to Nantucket by the name that distinguished her contribution to the war: "If Nantucket be not in truth the banner town in the work of raising men at her country's call, she must be very near that honorable rank." It was noted that Nantucket had made her great contribution from motives of pure patriotism at a time when the town was in economic straits, while other communities were deriving some benefits from the war. On Nantucket, whaling and fishing businesses had suffered, the shoe business had failed, and the school appropriation had been reduced, while other towns had prospered from increased revenues associated with the war. Despite these economic and social losses, Nantucket had never failed in recruiting or contributing freely to support the war.

The *Inquirer* carried an advertisement from a Boston committee to "Fill Up the Old Regiments!"—an attempt to fill the ranks of the early Massachusetts regiments that had lost so many men to battle and disease over the past three years. The recruiting system tended to favor new regiments rather than replenish the earlier ones, and the creation of new organizations offered more political rewards as new officers were appointed. The ad offered an extra bonus of "TEN DOLLARS . . . to any person bringing an accepted Recruit" to fill up the old Massachusetts infantry regiments of the 9th and 2nd Army Corps, commanded by Major Generals Burnside and Hancock, the latter commanding the 20th Massachusetts.

Gettysburg was remembered in March with the news that the bodies of the Union dead had been removed to appropriate places in the National Cemetery there. The number was 3,512, including almost a thousand unknown. The bodies of the Confederate dead were to be placed in a separate enclosure. It was noted that a monument would be raised near the spot where General John Reynolds fell. Officers who were home on leave were mentioned: Colonel George N. Macy, who lost his left hand at Gettysburg, and Captain John W. Summerhayes of the 20th Massachusetts came home; and Lieutenant Charles F. Folger 2nd, of the 27th Wisconsin Regiment, was home after serving under General Grant in the West.

The presidential campaign of 1864 started early, with partisan criticism of Abraham Lincoln and his conduct of the war, but the *Inquirer* called for the display of patriotic spirit and the utmost harmony in that time of crisis.

May of 1864 was filled with news from the front. The great army of General Grant began its move south of the Rapidan River to confront Robert E. Lee. For two weeks the public was consumed with excitement, looking to Grant as the savior of the Union and expecting great accomplishments.

Nantucket read about the battle of the Wilderness, in which Colonel George N. Macy was again wounded in the leg, and where Major Henry L. Abbott, former captain of Company I and in Macy's absence commander of the regiment, was killed on May 6. Abbott was noted for his bravery and coolness in battle, but he was unusually kind and solicitous toward his men. Learning that many of the families of the Nantucket men in Company I were in need, he contributed $100 of his own money to their relief, and in his last words to his father requested that whatever remained of his money should be used to help his Nantucket men and their families. Dying at the age of 22, Henry L. Abbott left a warm memory in the hearts of the Nantucket community. The wounded Colonel Macy accompanied the body of Major Abbott to Boston for a state funeral.

The next week brought news of the great clash of the armies at Spotsylvania, where the soldiers fought for twenty hours at point-blank range in rain and mud. The list of casualties mounted rapidly: Samuel C. Crocker and George B. Starbuck, wounded; Sergeant William P. Kelley (the great physical specimen) taken prisoner; Benjamin Wyer and Gorham Andrews of the 58th Massachusetts receiving wounds of the arms; and William R. Beard and George Spencer, Jr., killed.

Remote from the fields of battle, Nantucket waited anxiously for news of the war as Grant moved slowly south, his campaign understood to be a steady but costly success:

> The campaign has been a severe one; but our successes have been steady and tenacious. . . . Tuesday's mail brought us the news of our victories at Coal Harbor (Cold Harbor). Gen. Grant's forces met the enemy . . . again and again the rebels charged our troops, but were as often repulsed with great slaughter. Our entire loss in killed, wounded and missing during the three days' fighting around Coal Harbor, will not exceed 7500.

The grim tale of Cold Harbor was yet to be told to the eager readers of Nantucket. News to the island came from mainland papers, and was often delayed and distorted. Meanwhile the readers were told the army was in excellent spirits, and General Grant was the hero of the hour.

HOPES OF AN END TO THE WAR inspired dreams of the revival of Nantucket's dismal economy, with an article pushing "Nantucket as a Summer Resort." Noting the summer temperature at a mild 72 degrees (unless there is a fog), Nantucket was described as a tolerable place to sleep at night with open windows, with or without blankets. The quiet and cool climate, with the boundless and sublime ocean surrounding, were commended to those seeking relief from city life. This optimism was balanced by the news that the Atlantic Straw Works was going out of business, after ten years of trying to provide straw hats and employment to the women of the town.

The summer of 1864 featured the Sanitary Fair, an event sponsored by the women of Nantucket to provide funds and comforts for the Sanitary Commission, which served as the forerunner of the Red Cross. The Sanitary Fair opened in the Atheneum Hall with a prayer, a speech, and a round of varied entertainments, including auctions, fortune tellers, magic shows, and refreshments. Both the upper and lower floors of the Atheneum were filled with activities, and the public responded with generous attention to the ladies and their cause.

The fair opened at the Atheneum, then continued on to Pantheon Hall for three more evenings, with Miss Emily Shaw reading from Dickens's *Battle of Life,* illustrated by tableaux.

The Sanitary Fair wound up its events on a Monday, with gross receipts of $2,200 and a net gain after expenses of $1,800, which was considered a handsome sum for the relief of the sick and wounded. The fair was honored with a visit from several dignitaries including ex-Secretary of the Treasury (later Chief Justice) Salmon P. Chase; Congressman Samuel Hooper; the Honorable John Murray Forbes; Colonel Codman, late of the 45th Massachusetts; and Captain Mason of the 20th Massachusetts. The men arrived on a yacht, held an interview at the fair, and were then entertained at the mansion of Frederick C. Sanford before returning the next day to Cotuit.

Recruits for the army were sought in an advertisement inserted by the selectmen as recruiting agents to enlist volunteers, offering to those who joined before the draft a federal bounty of $100, and a state bounty of $325, payable $50 down and $20 per month during the term of service.

The first term of the regiment expired in July of 1864, and the remnants of the 20th Massachusetts who had not reenlisted for another three years arrived in Boston. Many Nantucket boys had served in Company I, and the ranks had been filled with local boys to replace those lost to battle or disease. The returning veterans were Patrick Conway, Josiah F. Murphey, Erwin H. Backus, George C. Pratt, George A. Backus, and William A. Barrett.

September brought more news of the election campaign and a copy of the Democratic platform, resolving "to preserve the Federal Union and the rights of the States unimpaired; and they declare they consider the Administrative usurpation of extraordinary and dangerous powers not granted by the Constitution. . . ." General George B. McClellan's letter of acceptance of the nomination was described as "accepting the nomination but rejecting the platform." The *Inquirer* gave a running account of McClellan's many retreats and failures and predicted the country would see his letter as "the stamp of the artful politician."The paper endorsed the Republican ticket of Lincoln and Johnson, and printed a letter from General Grant in which he stated, "I have no doubt but the enemy are exceedingly anxious to hold out until after the presidential election. . . . They hope for the election of a Peace candidate."

The men of Nantucket went to the polls for the November election leaving little doubt where Nantucket stood on the political scene. By identical votes of 487 to 35, they elected every single Republican candidate on the ballot, with Lincoln losing one voter and receiving 486 votes. It was noted the vote total was 77 less than in 1860, probably due to the loss of manpower during the war, but many old men showed up to vote for the first time in years. The *Inquirer* shouted: "Another good day's work is accomplished. By an immense majority the voters of Nantucket have declared for an undivided country, a policy which admits of no compromise with traitors, a vigorous prosecution of the war and a nation without a slave."

Late in November, the paper printed in full the story of General William T. Sherman's march through Georgia, including his famous order to the troops: "The army will forage liberally on the country during the march." The year ended with Sherman delivering the city of Savannah as a "Christmas present" to President Lincoln.

The final war story of the year was about David M. Folger, a native of Nantucket who had returned in December with the tale of his confinement with other local men in the dreaded prison at Andersonville. He returned in an exchange of prisoners through Savannah, miraculously unscathed, the only man among twenty-two comrades who had been captured in February who was known to have survived to the end of the year.

1865

THE YEAR 1865 BROUGHT TO NANTUCKET rumors of peace as the forces of Grant and Sherman gradually closed the net around the remaining rebel armies. In February, news of the fighting around Peters-

burg, with the 2nd Corps pressing the rebels at Hatcher's Run, provoked the comment that Grant was keeping Lee's army busy to prevent him from sending troops to oppose General Sherman's relentless
advance through the South. In the same month, three Confederate
commissioners met with President Lincoln at Fortress Monroe (on
the steamer *River Queen,* later to serve Nantucket on the run from
New Bedford), in Virginia, and submitted proposals for peace, which
proved fruitless. It was expected that Grant's final campaign would
be the most significant of the war.

In February, with victory in sight, the *Mirror* issued an unusually
strong editorial opposing a compromise peace. After the sacrifice of
300,000 loyal men, the national honor would not accept such a peace:

> This cannot be; this shall not be! We have no concession to make with the merciless
> leaders of the slave oligarchy; we desire to crush out, now and forever, the life and spir-
> it of the slave power. . . . Let us say to the South, with the hero of Vicksburg: "uncondi-
> tional surrender" is our claim; we demand it.

This new, aggressive spirit was engendered by the prospect of early
triumph and by the horrors described by Nantucket's former prisoners of war. News of the terrible conditions and inhumane treatment of men in the prison pens of Georgia and Virginia aroused a
demand for retaliation against rebel prisoners, but the *Inquirer* considered such harsh treatment a revolting act of vengeance that ill
became a civilized people.

Sergeant Albert P. Fisher of the 58th Massachusetts Volunteer Infantry
arrived home after six months' incarceration in the prisons at Salisbury (near Wilmington, North Carolina) and Libby (in Richmond,
Virginia). He had been taken prisoner on September 30, 1864. His
treatment at Salisbury had been shameful: he was stripped of his
clothing and robbed of everything he had, including a ring on his
finger. On several occasions at Salisbury, prisoners had been deprived
of food for thirty-six hours at a time. He named seven other Nantucket men who remained behind at Salisbury, some of whom did
not survive their confinement. Upon his return home, Fisher was
still feeble and emaciated.

Lieutenant Benjamin B. Pease of the 20th Massachusetts and George Christian of the 2nd Massachusetts Cavalry, having been prisoners at Danville, Virginia, also arrived home with their own tales of the prison camp. Nantucket could only hope and pray for the safe return of the men who were still confined in enemy prisons.

March brought the second inauguration of Abraham Lincoln, in the presence of thousands standing in knee-deep mud. Not since Andrew Jackson had a president been reelected, and Lincoln had done it while the Civil War raged. The ceremony took place without incident, in contrast to the ominous atmosphere of the 1861 inaugural. Recognizing the importance of the occasion, Lincoln delivered one of his most memorable speeches, and the *Mirror* saw fit to print the Second Inaugural Address in full.

On March 22, Alfred Macy, editor of the *Inquirer,* wrote his last editorial, announcing that the paper had been sold to the *Mirror*, whose owners would thereafter publish a new paper to be called the *Inquirer and Mirror.*

Citing the hopeful turn of events on the national scene—the ending of the rebellion, the victories of the armies, the reelection of Lincoln, and the abolition of slavery—the editor deemed it an appropriate time to bring the *Inquirer* to the conclusion of its role in Nantucket newspaper history. Realistically, the sale was attributable to the island's declining economic fortunes. Unlike some northern communities, Nantucket had not prospered during the Civil War; now more than ever, the island could support one newspaper at best. But the new paper would not stray far from the basic policies of its predecessors: "Nothing but loyalty to the constitution, and freedom," the acquiring *Mirror* announced, "can be tolerated."

April was full of momentous news for the first issues of the *Inquirer and Mirror*. News of the fall of Richmond arrived at four o'clock in the morning, when the noted Captain David G. Patterson arrived with his schooner *Passport*, bringing the news from Hyannis to the island.

The irrepressible town crier, Billy Clark, seized a copy of the Boston newspaper and raced around town with his horn in hand, blaring the good news of the capture of Richmond. The consolidated *Inquirer and Mirror,* starting at seven in the morning, produced an extra edition that was grabbed by the public as fast as the copies came off the press. Flags were raised and bells sounded across the old town, the school children were given the day off, and a thirty-five-gun salute was fired off at noon. That night, the façade of Engine Company No. 8 was illuminated, and the joyous townspeople danced in the streets.

The editor published the "glorious news" with a note of cheer mixed with prophecy:

> This has been a war, not for this generation alone, but for myriads yet unborn. . . . In its result depends the interest of all to whom liberty is dear in foreign lands, now and in all future time. In our failure would have been buried the hope of the race. The experiment, as it has been slightingly termed, would have failed; and men would not again have pointed to America as the city set on a hill, the wonder and pride of the nations.

Amid the rejoicing came news of the death of Seth C. Chase, of the 39th Massachusetts, who died at his home in Nantucket only three weeks after returning from six months in the prisons of Libby and Salisbury, where he contracted the disease that killed him.

Saturday, April 15, was the day Lincoln died, but the *Inquirer and Mirror*, without a wireless service, went to press without knowing of the tragedy. Its headline read "The Union Triumphant!" and it announced the surrender of General Lee and described the fall of Richmond with unrestrained joy: "Glory! Hallelujah!" Grant, Sherman, and Sheridan had won the admiration of the world, and the soldiers had covered themselves with glory, The fall of the Confederacy coincided with the finishing of the Capitol dome in Washington, rising as "a mountain of hope in the blue of Heaven"—another event that symbolized the triumph of the Union.

The fall of Richmond, it was noted, was due in great part to the efforts of General Weitzel and his colored brigades. Capture of Richmond by the black troops was especially gratifying to Massachusetts' wartime governor, John A. Andrew, who had long espoused their cause, and wired Secretary of War Stanton: "The colored men, received late, got in first, and thus is the Scripture fulfilled."

From boundless joy to the depths of sorrow, the next issue of the paper was edged in black and led with the story of "The National Grief." In Nantucket, all public buildings were draped in mourning and the flags of the fleet were at half mast. The Unitarian and Congregationalist ministers joined in a community service at the North Church. The paper reported the details of the assassination in full. The grief of the community was profound, for there was never any American more admired on Nantucket than Abraham Lincoln.

After the death of Lincoln, the hope for the future was a reflection of confidence in the Union. The *Inquirer and Mirror* doubtless spoke for most of the community:

> This is a government not of men but of principles. The leaders are but exponents of those principles. Thrice is he armed who hath his quarrel just. When the helmsman is stricken down, the vessel may for a moment swerve from her course, but a new hand at the wheel, with his eye on the compass, and informed by the chart, will direct her safely.

EPILOGUE

THE MEN FROM NANTUCKET who returned from the war came home to a town whose fortunes had declined but whose strength of character was undiminished. Nantucket had earned its place as the "Banner Town" of the Commonwealth, and it was proud of its service to the Union cause. The veterans soon formed a local post of the Grand Army of the Republic and its members were honored men in the community. The first monument ever erected on the island was the Civil War memorial to the seventy-three men who gave their lives during the conflict.

The island itself was still in the economic depression that had begun before the war: the population dropped from 6,094 in 1860 to 4,830 in 1865, and would fall to 4,123 in 1870. The remnants of the whaling fleet disappeared and every industry attempted as a replacement failed. The prosperity that had resulted from wartime business in many Massachusetts cities—where industries produced shoes, uniforms, and arms for the troops—completely bypassed the island community. A feeling of isolation and helplessness pervaded the town.

It was the fate of Nantucket's war veterans to accept and make the best of their hometown prospects. Josiah F. Murphey came home to find his old job at the Union Store, after unsuccessfully seeking employment in the shoe industry in Brockton. George Nelson Macy, the only general in Nantucket's history, returned to his position at the Suffolk Savings Bank in Boston. John W. Summerhayes rejoined as an officer in the regular army, where he spent a long career as an Indian fighter. Most of the farmers and fishermen returned to their former occupations.

In many ways, the Civil War years represented the island's last great community effort, when Nantucketers were united in a task fully as awesome as that accomplished during the glory days of whaling. Sharing the spirit and dedication and united purpose of the whaling families, the men and women of Nantucket determined to give their utmost effort to the cause of preserving the Union. The same men whose forebears had withstood the terrors of the whale's attack did not flinch from the guns of Gettysburg. Their wives and mothers endured the long years of loneliness and loss that the women of Nantucket had known in earlier times, and their spirit inspired the men to do their duty.

Edouard A. Stackpole, Nantucket's eminent historian, remembered how the men of the G.A.R. used to gather every year at the corner of Main and Federal streets for the Memorial Day parade. At first, there were many veterans, and they did not make much of the event; but as the years passed and there were fewer comrades left, they seemed to realize what they had done and took more pride in their accomplishments. As Stackpole remembered, "They seemed to stand a little taller each year."

APPENDIX

The 20th Massachusetts at Gettysburg

THE 20TH MASSACHUSETTS VOLUNTEER INFANTRY arrived at Gettysburg late on July 1, 1863, with the 2nd Corps commanded by General Winfield Scott Hancock. The regimental commander was Colonel Paul Joseph Revere, with Lieutenant Colonel George Nelson Macy second in command. Upon arrival, the 20th was placed in position as part of the 3rd Brigade, under Colonel Norman Hall, part of the 2nd Division under the command of General John B. Gibbon.

On July 2, the position of the 20th was in the front line of infantry on Cemetery Ridge, near the left center of the Union Line, about 100 yards south of the "Clump of Trees" that became the object of Pickett's Charge on July 3. It was about 200 yards south of the Angle, the corner of the stone wall where the Confederates were to strike the Union line.

The Union infantry was stationed behind a stone and rail fence—actually a split-rail wooden fence atop a low wall of stones—an arrangement known locally as "cow high and hog low," which provided ideal cover for the troops.

[The position of the 20th Massachusetts is today marked by a large monument made of Roxbury puddingstone in the shape of an irregular boulder, a gift of the Commonwealth of Massachusetts in 1886. The left and right flanks of the regiment are delineated by small stone markers about thirty yards apart. Directly behind the marker for the 20th stand the markers for the 19th Massachusetts, which backed up the forward line of defenders.]

From its position on Cemetery Ridge, the 20th had an unobstructed view across the valley toward the woods on Seminary Ridge, with the red barn of the Codori Farm on the Emmitsburg Road standing slightly to the left. This position was the original object of the charge led by General George Pickett from the right flank of the Confederate line toward the Clump of Trees.

On the second day of the battle, the 20th was largely inactive in the center of the Union line, holding its position under a broiling sun while the enemy struck heavy blows on the right and left flanks of the Union position. Late in the day, however, a stray shell burst in their ranks and killed Colonel Revere, after which command devolved upon Lieutenant Colonel George Nelson Macy.

It was on that day that the men watched with intense interest the battle raging on their left flank, where the Mississippi Brigade, whom they had faced at Fredericksburg, stormed through the Peach Orchard and the Wheatfield, to its destruction and the death of General William Barksdale.

As the final day of battle dawned on July 3, General John B. Gibbon warned his troops that the next Confederate attack would strike the center of their line. He ordered his men to lie low and hold their fire until the rebels were close, then "fire fast and low." Lying still and sweltering under a hot sun, the men waited.

At about noontime, the Federal troops watched a historic dinner party, as the Union generals gathered to eat a meal in the open. Using an old mess chest as a table, Generals Hancock and Gibbon sat down to eat a frugal meal, later described as "a very old chicken." General Meade rode up and was invited to join the party, being given a seat on a cracker box. Then Generals John Newton and Alfred Pleasanton came up and were invited to sit on the ground. When the last bone was picked clean, the generals lighted cigars and the party broke up. A veteran chicken had done its duty for the Army of the Republic.

Toward one o'clock the massed Confederate artillery on Seminary Ridge commenced a cannonade aimed at the center of the Union line that lasted two hours. Fortunately, the aim was high and little damage was done to the infantry hugging the ground, but great havoc was done among the horses and supply wagons behind the forward lines, where 250 horses were killed. General Henry Hunt, commander of the federal artillery, answered the Confederate guns for awhile, then decided to silence his guns to save ammunition and provoke the Confederate infantry to attack. This led the Confederates to conclude that their artillery barrage had been successful and the time had arrived to order the infantry charge.

Around three o'clock, with the guns silent, the massed infantry of Pickett's Charge emerged from the woods, and 13,000 men in perfect formation, with flags flying and bands playing, started forward. The spectacle of this massed military display created a moment that men remembered for the rest of their lives.

The rebels were permitted to approach within rifle range, then the Union defenders rose and began to deliver a deadly fire into the enemy ranks. Standing behind their stone wall to blast the Confederates crossing the open field toward their entrenched position, the Union men immediately saw the comparison with the battlefield of the past December and began to shout, "Fredericksburg! Fredericksburg!"

As they headed toward the Clump of Trees, the Confederates were pressed to the left by artillery fire from Cemetery Ridge and the flanking fire of General Stannard's Vermont Brigade. Thus they struck the line north of the Massachusetts position near the Angle of the stone fence, breaking two Pennsylvania regiments. Immediately, all the Union forces on the ridge responded to the breakthrough, rushing to the point of attack without waiting for orders.

Lieutenant Colonel George Nelson Macy and Lieutenant Henry L. Abbott sent their men to the right, crashing into the rebel attack and piling into the affray with rifles, swords, and bayonets. Amid all the noise, smoke, and turmoil, no orders could be heard and each man fought in his own way, knowing this battle must be won.

The desperate struggle lasted about thirty minutes. Rebels reached the Union battery commanded by Lieutenant Alonzo H. Cushing, who fired one last round and died by his guns. Confederate General Lewis A. Armistead, waving his hat atop his sword, strode over the stone wall, put his hand on one of the Union cannon, and fell mortally wounded. His death marked the beginning of the end for the Confederacy.

Lieutenant Colonel George Nelson Macy went down, his left hand shattered by a minié ball, and Lieutenant Abbott took command of the regiment. When the rebel tide receded, the field was covered with dead and wounded men; 1400 Confederates had surrendered, and every one of their generals, except Pickett, had been killed or wounded. Henry L. Abbott wrote: "The rows of dead after the battle I found to be 15 and 20 feet apart; as near to hand to hand fighting as I ever care to see."

Among the 20th Massachusetts, seven company commanders had been killed or wounded, thirty-one men killed, and ninety-three wounded. Of the Nantucketers, Henry Jones was dead at the age of eighteen and William Barrett, Daniel Chase, Samuel Christian, Benjamin Pease, and Arthur Rivers were wounded. Lieutenant Colonel Macy suffered wounds that required the amputation of his left hand.

Despite their enormous losses, the survivors of Gettysburg in the 20th Massachusetts remained confident, maintaining a high standard of discipline and pride, a tribute to the loyalty of the men and the quality of the officers.

Henry L. Abbott summed it up: "It was worth all our defeats."

1 Leander F. Alley, 1834–62. Here in uniform of a private, probably 1861, he was commissioned second lieutenant in the field and was killed at Fredericksburg.

2 Josiah Fitch Murphey, having recovered from typhoid fever contracted in
August 1863, after the battle of Fredericksburg.

3 Brevet Major General George Nelson Macy, ca. 1865, Nantucket's highest ranking officer in the Civil War.

4 John W. Summerhayes, ca. 1890. Major in the 20th Massachusetts; here as lieutenant colonel in postwar regular army.

5 Elisha Pope Fearing Gardner. "Elisha in the uniform he wore as General Butler's spy," as labeled on back of photograph, ca. 1900.

6 The Union Store, Main Street, Nantucket, ca 1890, where Murphey worked before and after the war.

7 Thomas M. Gardner Post 207, Grand Army of the Republic, ca. 1917.

8 Josiah Fitch Murphey, aged 74, in G.A.R. uniform, showing facial scar from
wounding at Fredericksburg (photograph marked by Murphey).

9 The Civil War Monument, erected on upper Main Street in 1874, bearing the names of the seventy-three Nantucket men who lost their lives.

II Biographical Notes on Josiah Fitch Murphey

Josiah F. Murphey: A Raw Recruit

ON AUGUST 12, 1862, a nineteen-year-old grocery clerk named Josiah Fitch Murphey walked up the stairs at Pantheon Hall on Nantucket's Main Street and enlisted in Company I of the 20th Massachusetts Volunteer Infantry. Full of patriotic enthusiasm, he sang en route to boot camp:

> I'm a raw recruit with a bran[d] new suit
> One hundred dollars bounty.
> I'm going down to Washington,
> To fight for Nantucket County.

Murphey did not choose the 20th Massachusetts because of its Harvard-educated, blue-blooded officer corps or its combat record. Like hundreds of thousands of boys, North and South, he simply chose to wage his war in the company of friends, neighbors, and, in his case, an older brother by sixteen years, Franklin Barnard Murphey. Company I, one of ten companies composing the regiment, had a large Nantucket contingent raised the previous summer by islander and later Brevet Major General George Nelson Macy. By war's end, eighty Nantucketers had composed about one-third of Company I's total enrollment.

Forty-seven of the men had enlisted with Murphey in the summer of 1862. Of those, eight would be killed in action or mortally wounded, ten would be wounded, three would die from disease, four would become prisoners of war (of whom three would die in captivity), and sixteen others (excluding those discharged because of wounds) would be discharged from the army because of accident or disease. In short, only six of the "Summer of '62" recruits would return unscathed.

Josiah Murphey would not be one of them. Although he survived his two-year term, it would be a close call on at least two occasions: he was shot in the face at the battle of Fredericksburg and six months later survived a long bout with typhoid fever. It was no surprise, then, that when his enlistment expired and the Army of the Potomac's war still raged in the trenches outside Petersburg, Virginia, Murphey rejected the offer of an officer's commission if he would reenlist. "I did not choose to remain," he confided thirty years afterward, "[as] it was too hard a life for me."

His life during those two years is the subject of his memoirs. Written in 1895–96, his reminiscing was prompted in part by Arthur H. Gardner, a state legislator from Nantucket and editor of the short-lived Nantucket *Journal*. In the 1890s, Gardner sensed the revival of national interest in Civil War history and published a series of articles by Nantucket's Civil War veterans. Appearing during the winter of 1895–96 they ultimately numbered twenty-two articles by veterans who had served in eight Union regiments or the United States Navy. Murphey's contribution—describing camp life, his baptism by fire at Antietam, and the slaughter of his company in the streets of Fredericksburg in the frigid dusk of December 11, 1862—is included in his memoirs.

But Murphey added much more. His memoirs include numerous anecdotes about his army experiences as well as a diary he kept while on the march from the battle of the Wilderness to the gates of Petersburg. His timing in gathering those records was not coincidental. Renewal of interest in the Civil War had come to Nantucket as well as the nation. It was sparked in part by a resurgence in membership and power of the Grand Army of the Republic, or G.A.R., the principal Union Civil War veterans' organization. The G.A.R. was dedicated to enshrining a war that had been the most important experience of Josiah F. Murphey's life, and he would help reestablish that organization on Nantucket.

Shortly after the war, a G.A.R. post was founded on the island with Josiah F. Murphey as a member. However, as interest in a war that had been a national obsession since 1861 had declined, so had G.A.R. membership throughout the country, and no more so than on Nantucket. In 1874 the Nantucket G.A.R. disbanded. By 1885, Memorial Day was not even being observed on the island.

That changed by 1890, and in 1891 the Nantucket G.A.R. was founded anew, becoming the Thomas M. Gardner Post 207 of the Grand Army of the Republic. Forty-eight-year-old Josiah Murphey was a founding member, and by 1920 he had served seven terms as its post commander.

With the reinvigoration of the G.A.R. came a national campaign for members to preserve for posterity their wartime experiences. Called "personal war sketches" (Murphey calls his "a short sketch of my life in the army"), they were collected and kept in large books available to post members. As far as is known, Murphey's memoirs and diary are the only such record that survives of the Nantucket G.A.R.

JOSIAH FITCH MURPHEY was born on Nantucket on January 12, 1843, the youngest of six children of Captain Charles and Sarah Murphey. Josiah's paternal great-grandfather was the first Nantucket Murphey and appears as "James Murphey of Ireland" in a local genealogy. Tradition has it that James arrived on the island about 1750 when his ship foundered off shore near Siasconset, a fishing village on Nantucket's eastern coast. He remained on island, married, had children, and died there in 1775.

Like many Nantucketers, Murphey's father looked to the sea for his livelihood. He was third mate on the whaler *Dauphin* when it rescued two survivors of the *Essex*, the ship that had been destroyed by a whale and is thought to have inspired Herman Melville's *Moby-Dick*. What Charles Murphey did next was something extraordinary for a third mate on any vessel. He versified the *Dauphin*'s logbook in 220 rhyming stanzas. Published in 1877, *A Journal of a Whaling Voyage on Board Ship* Dauphin, relates of the *Essex:*

> The second month, quite early on
> The three-and-twentieth day,
> From our mast-head we did espy
> A boat to leeward way.
>
> Hard up the helm, and down we went
> To see who it might be.
> The Essex boat we found it was,
> Been ninety days at sea.
>
> No victuals were there in the boat,
> Of any sort or kind,
> And two survivors, who did expect
> A watery grave to find.

His long poem concludes after the *Dauphin* has returned to Nantucket laden with whale oil:

> Our oil is sold, and cash is paid;
> We'll share it with our friends,
> And when it's gone, to sea once more.
> And so my voyage ends.

WHEN CAPTAIN CHARLES MURPHEY died at the age of 59 in 1859, he was remembered less as a whaler than as a man who filled several local public offices with great distinction. The Nantucket *Weekly Mirror* took the unusual step of publishing his obituary in its editorial columns. The accolades describe a *beau idéal* of nineteenth-century American civilization:

> For many years, Captain Murphey has had the custody of several of our public buildings and offices, and has been a general agent for the distribution of papers and notices, and for the collection of money, and he has been without exception, honest in his collections and payments, careful and prompt in the custody and preparation of our public halls, persevering, yet not obtrusive in the collection of bills, and courteous in his deportment upon all occasions. Captain Murphey had virtues of a higher grade than even these. He was temperate, charitable in judgment, and benevolent in action, contributing from his moderate store to the wants of the unfortunate. Who of us can lay aught to his charge?

Josiah Murphey's mother, Sarah, was a Barnard, a Nantucket Quaker family dating from the earliest white settlements of the island. As is regrettably the case too often in assessing the influence and role of women on persons and events, little is known about her. She was the last of thirteen children, eleven of whom reached maturity. When she died at the age of 95 in 1895, she was the oldest living Nantucketer. Observing that she "retained her faculties in a surprising degree," her obituarist noted her excellence in fancy needlework and knitting, and that her work was "awarded a premium" during a recent county fair.

Just as little is known of Josiah Murphey's life before the war. He attended Nantucket High School but left at the age of fifteen, the year his father died. His father's obituary suggests modest means, and perhaps that was what prompted Murphey to work as a clerk at the Union Store, a grocery near the corner of Main and Centre streets.

Nonetheless, what education he did receive served him well. His writing style is straightforward, occasionally eloquent, and like his father's, possessed of a sense of humor. While literacy would be essential for Murphey's terms of service as postmaster, town clerk, town assessor, and commander of the Nantucket G.A.R., his sense of humor would help him to survive the Civil War.

JOSIAH MURPHEY'S BATTLE ITINERARY between August 1862 and July 1864 is that of his regiment. The only notable exception was Gettysburg. En route to that historic engagement he contracted typhoid fever and was hospitalized for several months in Washington, D.C. Before July 1863, he participated in the battle of Second Manassas, the Maryland Campaign, Fredericksburg, and Chancellorsville. Afterward, he stood at Mine Run, the Wilderness Campaign, and, finally, the investment of Petersburg. His combat experience and life in the army are the sole subject of his memoirs and diary. Murphey speaks well for himself, and needs no reprise from a desk-bound historian one hundred and thirty years later.

But much has changed over the last century in the way historians have come to view the Civil War. The emphasis has shifted from the general's headquarters tent to the dog tents of the ranks. Over the past two decades, Civil War historiography has attempted to open the haversacks and knapsacks of the common soldier, and to question who he was, why he fought, and how army life and combat changed him.

Josiah Murphey has something to contribute to the discussion. His words yield important insights into the psychology of the approximately two million Billy Yanks who passed through the ranks of the Union army between the years 1861 and 1865. Historians' attention has recently focused on the clash between the citizen-soldier's expectations of army life and the reality he encountered on the battlefield; how he adjusted to ubiquitous death at its most grotesque and how he coped with the ineptitude of commanders and with the enemy responsible for that death. Murphey's memoirs reveal a boy caught up in the fascination and horror of war. They also shed light on the subtle psychological adjustments required to survive an experience that left few unscarred.

Murphey had much in common with many northern recruits when he enlisted. Although the average age of Civil War soldiers was just under 26, the largest single age group was 18. Like the "statistical recruit," Murphey was raised in an isolated, rural or semirural community. He had high expectations of army life and the war he had volunteered to fight. It is no surprise that an early theme in his memoirs treats of his disappointment when confronted with the reality of that life.

He first encountered the reality at Camp Cameron, a collection and training facility for recruits bound for regiments already in the field. Situated in North Cambridge, Massachusetts, Cameron was described by Murphey as "a hard place where we really began to see something of the life of a soldier." He was struck by its size. With 5,000 men concentrated on fifty acres, its population approached that of Nantucket. But unlike Nantucket, in Camp Cameron "there were men of every nationality," no doubt referring to the English, Irish, German, and other foreign-born soldiers who would eventually comprise twenty percent of the Union army. He also discovered that not every recruit was as excited as he about fighting for their respective counties. He observed that the guards around the camp had only one purpose: "To keep the men in."

Their indoctrination was astonishing compared with modern military training: Murphey was in boot camp only two weeks, and was not issued a rifle. On August 29, without a rifle, he reported to the 20th Massachusetts then encamped at Alexandria, Virginia. Disappointment followed him. "We met with the Nantucket boys who had come out about a year previous," he wrote, "and they told us that they were having a hard time marching and fighting." When Murphey enlisted, he had been told to expect "tents to sleep in and the best of medical attendance." Now at the seat of the war, he found things quite different: ". . . all the tent we should have would be what we could carry, that our bed would be the cold ground and our covering would be what blankets we could carry."

Later, he would have ample opportunity to decide for himself whether Civil War medical care was the best available; he does not spare the reader any details in his graphic accounts of field and Washington, D.C., military hospitals.

For Murphey, the harsh realities of campaigning began the day after he reported to his regiment. In a forced march that Murphey declared was "one of the hardest it was ever my lot to perform," he and the 20th Massachusetts walked thirty miles under a blazing Virginia sun to help cover Union General John Pope's retreat from the Federal disaster at Second Manassas. The march ended at midnight, and Murphey practically collapsed from exhaustion. During the march, he participated in a ritual of the Civil War army novitiate—"simmering down," abandoning along the road excess gear that burdened the march. Shed too were his civilian expectations of war and army life.

The ultimate experience of any soldier is combat, and two weeks later, Murphey received his baptismal fire standing with his regiment at Antietam Creek. En route, they passed the battlefield of South Mountain where they were held in reserve. There he saw Confederate dead for the first time, and the first thing he did was to "cut the buttons from their clothes to send home as mementoes." This bit of *sang froid* seems out of character for him, and perhaps feeling some revulsion, he says in the same paragraph:

> As we marched along the road, we passed several Rebs laying on the sides who had given out. [We] gave them a word of cheer by telling them that our ambulances would shortly be along and take them in the hospital [where] they would be treated the same as our own men.

Remembering Antietam thirty years later, Murphey described his first experience in combat as a "thrilling time." He seemed caught up, as some were, in the *sound* of it all. Adrenalin flowing, he recalled "The roar of musketry and artillery, the bursting of shells, the commands of the officers mingled with the shrieks and groans of the wounded."

But it is just as likely that Murphey's first sight of the elephant ("seeing the elephant" was a term used by both sides in the conflict to describe combat duty) was something less than thrilling. According to the late Edouard Stackpole, dean of Nantucket historians, as the 20th Massachusetts stood at Antietam preparing for action in an early morning fog, they were unable to see the enemy although receiving his fire. When the fog lifted, Murphey saw that his brother Franklin had fallen only a few yards away. When Josiah broke ranks to help his brother, he was forced back into line by a diligent file closer, whose job it was to keep the men in the ranks and to prevent desertion and rout. As the line of battle advanced, he was forced to abandon his brother on the field.

At the end of the battle, Murphey returned to the field and observed things less "thrilling" than had been the case just a few hours before. The trampled corn was now joined by "regular rows" of Confederate dead lying "just as they had fallen." There was no more talk about cutting buttons from the corpses for mementos, and one senses a horror creeping into his words as he describes how the rebels "would make a stand for a while, fall back and make another and their line of dead showed where each had been made." Murphey's fixation with physical death, present throughout his memoirs, was just beginning.

Could it have been otherwise? Peaceful men thrust into warfare, with its irrational and anonymously distributed death are likely to experience profound dehumanization as they struggle to cope with battlefields paved for miles with the mangled and dead. It was certainly so with Murphey. His memoirs are replete with ghastly accounts of death and wounds. He understood all too well that war is about killing in its most physical sense. He reveals a fascination with those whose skulls have been emptied of brains by a random shell. But it is a detached fascination, as if the victim is somehow less human, and very distant from Murphey, who himself was cowering in a trench or a hospital bed just a few yards away, calculating the odds.

He spares his readers few details. His hospital experiences abound with piles of amputated limbs and dreadful accounts of operations and autopsies. And on June 24, 1864, in the trenches outside Petersburg, he records the appalling effects that an artillery shell caused among several comrades just a few feet away:

> . . . of the two killed one had the back of his head blown completely off with his brains taken entirely out and scattered over everybody near him. The other had a large part of his left side torn off. . . . Those near were compelled to wipe their gun and clothes with bunches of grass of the blood and brains of their comrades.

Yet his diary entry for that day closes with observations that point to a fundamental contradiction in Murphey and all those forced by circumstance to dehumanize others as well as themselves—on some level, *they* remain human. Murphey's sense of helplessness and his need to repress what he has seen abound: "I have seen many terrible and ghastly sights on the field of battle," he says, "men with an arm or a leg torn entirely off, heads shattered in all forms, but such things are to horrible to talk about, such is war with all its terrible consequences."

How Murphey resolves this tension between the dehumanizing realities of war and his own humanity is an important and reassuring theme that appears in different guises throughout his writings. He jokes and argues politics with captured Confederates in the aftermath of the Union disaster at Fredericksburg (shortly after his own hideous wounding) and during the bloodbath of Spotsylvania. On picket duty by the Rappahannock River during the winter of 1862–63, he approvingly relates another curious but almost universal ritual practiced by the ranks between battles during the Civil War:

> While in this camp our men would shout across to the johnnies to bring over some tobacco and swap for coffee and they would meet half way in the river and exchange coffee for tobacco and also exchange papers. We were within rifle range of each other all winter and spring, but no firing was done across the river.

The conflict between the demands of war and his own need for human contact is most poignantly expressed in his diary entry of June 6, 1864, following the awful carnage of Cold Harbor. Three days after the battle, as the stench of the dead choked the survivors, a burial truce was at last arranged, and Murphey observed "each side jump on their works without their guns and look at each other and all I can think of is mosquitoes. . . ." Yet the truce lasts long enough so that the "mosquitoes" become something else:

> We gradually grow bolder and finally advance towards one another, and while the stretcher bearers are carrying off the wounded and men detailed are burying dead, we exchange [with the rebels] the daily papers.

This brief respite from the killing exercised a powerful hold on the combatants. "Our flag of truce time has expired," he notes on June 8, "but we still expose ourselves and the rebs do the same, and no firing is being carried on." In fact, by common consent of the ranks, this unofficial truce was extended for three days, and when hostilities resumed, it was as if among friends. Murphey's diary entry for June 9 notes this weird relationship: "This morning opened as usual the past three days without any firing and we exchanged papers but after 9 O'clock the rebs told us to get under cover and the skirmishing began again."

Another important theme appearing throughout Murphey's memoirs and diary is his view that the sufferings of war are inevitable and beyond his ability to influence or change. In his diary, accounts of his privations are sometimes followed by his observation that "such is war, cruel resistless war." On one occasion, when the combination of a wet uniform, freezing temperatures, no wood for a campfire, and inadequate tenting made things "certainly uncomfortable," he excused what others might lay at the doorstep of inefficient officers and quartermasters with the comment that "such is a soldier's life and it was no use to grumble."

Again, on the eve of the battle of Fredericksburg, Murphey and several comrades gazed across the Rappahannock River at Lee's fortifications and discussed a truth that was plain in the mind of every private, if not in that of the commanding general Ambrose E. Burnside: if they were to be ordered to a frontal assault on those works (and they were), in Murphey's words, "many of us would never see the light of another day." But at the time he does not criticize General Burnside, whose stupidity lay behind the incipient Union disaster, nor does he criticize President Lincoln, the man who appointed Burnside. Instead, he closes the discussion by quietly noting that "we were soldiers and must take our chances."

Except for the burst of patriotism that opens his memoirs, his writings are mostly devoid of political comment or attempts to analyze or fix blame on others for the sufferings he daily endured. After a Confederate sniper shot him in the face at Fredericksburg, Murphey refused to blame even him. Drenched in his own blood, Murphey awoke and began to curse the "whole southern confederacy from Virginia to the gulf of Mexico." But not for long. "I realized it was war," he admonished himself, "and banished such thoughts from my mind."

It is this trait that finally distinguishes Josiah F. Murphey as an appealing human being. In spite of his immersion in sanctioned murder on a stupendous scale, his simple humanity triumphs above everything around him. Even in line of battle while taking and returning fire, when a comrade is killed, Murphey kneels to cover the man's face with the cape of the dead man's greatcoat. In the end, the vacant stares of the dead still move him.

His comrades certainly detected in him some special sensitivity. When fellow Nantucketer Lieutenant Leander F. Alley was killed at the battle of Fredericksburg, the wounded Murphey is chosen by Company I Captain Henry Livermore Abbott to accompany the body home and to personally relate to Alley's mother the details of her son's death.

Part of Murphey's appeal is his possession of the ultimate coping mechanism—an unflagging sense of humor. It intervenes at the most critical moments. In the field hospital at Fredericksburg, surrounded by the groans of the wounded and dying and the growing pile of amputated limbs, he befriends a wounded Confederate prisoner, a member of a regiment that had just inflicted the greatest number of casualties that Company I would suffer during the entire war. Murphey describes him as a "bright fellow and I talked with him many hours about the war and its causes." In the midst of this banter, he wryly passes on the Mississippian's suggestion that things would be easier if just Massachusetts and South Carolina would fight the war out.

Shortly afterward, a wounded Nantucketer in extreme pain was carried in on a stretcher. "He begged me piteously to kill him and end his sufferings," Murphey records. By the next morning, and with the help of opiates, the man's pain was gone. But Murphey couldn't resist asking him if he still wanted him to honor his request of the night before.

In the battle of the Wilderness, while ducking a hail of enemy lead, he observes an argument between two men as to who will carry the colors. The matter is settled when a bullet severs the staff. Several days later, he takes a Georgian prisoner, and the two boys debate the respective merits of Generals Grant and Lee. At Spotsylvania, he wryly records a moment of unfulfilled glory:

> I thought possible I might start the boys on a charge to dislodge [the rebels] as we were losing men fast . . . and gaining nothing. I seized my cap and running out in front of our line cried out, "Lets charge up there and drive them out!" But I could not start them and the firing continued as before.

Murphey's world abounds with a humorist's ironies. General Grant passes Murphey's regiment one night, and the men cheer so loudly that nearby Confederates mistake it for a Union attack and fire a volley into the ether. The Union commissary shoots and misses at a beef-ox meant for dinner; the frightened animal starts to cross the Rappahannock River toward Confederate lines when the frantic shouting of hungry rebel pickets terrifies the animal into returning to Union lines. Murphey personally delivers a message to Brigade Commander Alexander Webb, and ignores the general's warnings about a nearby sniper:

> Genl. Webb said to me, "Sergeant, you will get hit by a sharpshooter if you return that way. I said, "No, I guess not. I came that way and was not fired at," and I started and when I got about one quarter of the way across an open field I saw a puff of smoke and a bullet struck the ground near me and before I could pop down two or three more followed in quick succession. I immediately ran under cover of some bushes and the fireing ceased. I looked at the Genl. and he was watching me. I waved my hand to him and kept under cover until I reached the regiment in the breastworks. It was the only time that I could really say that I stood alone and was made a special target of by sharpshooters.

On July 18, 1864, his term expired, Josiah F. Murphey left the trenches of Petersburg for Boston and mustering out. His recollection of Nantucket's prewar business depression was very fresh. Before returning home he stopped in North Bridgewater (now Brockton), Massachusetts, seeking work as a shoemaker. Finding none, he returned to Nantucket and his old position at the Union Store.

Murphey joined the first incarnation of the Nantucket G.A.R. in

1868, and two years later married Avis Nelson Folger. He began receiving his pension during those years for his Fredericksburg wound. The minié ball had entered his cheek an inch below his right eye, and had exited about two inches to the right. It had left a deep scar and impaired vision.

Murphey bore this scar with pride. He appeared to the community as a man who, as Stackpole once related, "would stand a little taller each year" at Memorial Day commemorations. But there were other scars carried by the old veteran. A great-grandson who as a boy lived with Murphey remembers being awakened on several occasions by the night-time screams of the old man sleeping just down the hall. A parent patiently explained that Great-Grandfather was just having another dream about the war. The psychological trauma caused by war has gone by different names in different wars—shell shock, battle fatigue, and delayed stress syndrome. At the time of the Civil War, the world knew too little to name it.

In the years after the war, Murphey worked at a variety of jobs. He manufactured linen coats and assisted his father-in-law behind a butcher's counter. For a time he owned and operated a hardware store on Main Street across from the Pacific National Bank. But like his father, Murphey was best remembered for the public offices he held over many years. Entering middle age, he served as postmaster from 1879 to 1887. First elected as clerk of courts in 1888, he held that position until 1916. He was a town auditor from 1890 to 1902 and served on the board of assessors from 1902 to 1910.

A rare look at Murphey in his seniority attests to the respect and affection he enjoyed from his fellow Nantucketers. An article written by the mayor of Salem, Massachusetts, for the Salem *Dispatch* in 1910 described a recent visit to Nantucket. The correspondent tells of an unusual sixty-seven-year-old man he met while there:

> We were introduced to a certain "Uncle Cy," an uncle of our host. He was a native Nantucketer and although an old Civil War veteran, rode a bicycle and bathed in the surf. Uncle Cy is a marvel. We asked him questions galore about Nantucket people and he answered every one of them. He holds some town position like town clerk, but we

doubt if he ever refers to the books. As we were with him, people constantly asked him questions and he never once failed to give a correct answer. He knew people, names, dates, occurrences, marriages, deaths and births. He did not trouble to take people to his office, he just scratched his head and it came to him. Uncle Cy would make an ideal hotel clerk. We venture to predict that even in the Waldorf-Astoria with its six hundred arrivals a day, he would be the same satisfactory official as he is in little old Nantucket.

ON MAY 2, 1931, AT THE AGE OF 88, Josiah Fitch Murphey joined the permanent ranks of his beloved Army of the Potomac. The *Inquirer and Mirror* obituary used phrases such as "sterling citizen," "won the admiration of the entire community," and "won and held the respect of his fellow townsmen." But one suspects that Murphey, veteran of so many battles in so bloody a war, might have seen himself in a light not visible to any save other veterans of that conflict. Two years before his death, in a hand shaking with age, he wrote: "Boston Herald said [after the battle of Fredericksburg] that Murphey who was reported yesterday mortally wounded might possibly recover. He did and lived to be over 85 years old. He is writing this."

EDITORIAL NOTE

Murphey's memoirs, transcribed diaries, and newspaper articles are presented substantially as he wrote them. Punctuation has been changed in a few places and paragraphs broken for ease of reading. Otherwise, all of Murphey's deviations from standard grammar and spelling, including proper names and place names, are preserved.

III Josiah Fitch Murphey:
Memoirs of Service
in the Civil War,
with Diary Entries

The following pages in this book give a short sketch of my life in the army in the late War of the Rebellion, 1861-5 while I was a member of Company I. 20th Regt. Mass. Vol. Inf., attached to the third brigade Second division Second army Corps. and always with the Army of the Potomac commanded by Genl's Pope, M'Lellan, Burnside, Hooker, Meade and Grant covering a period of about two years. I enlisted as a Private and rose to the rank of acting Orderly Sergeant,[1] about the same as having a Lieutenant commission offered to me if I would *re-enlist* but I did not choose to remain, it was too hard a life for me.[2]

  As an appendix I have added a few short stories written from personal observations.

This history was written in the winter of 1895-6.

S/Josiah F. Murphey.

The following pages in this book give a short sketch of my life in the army in the late War of the Rebellion, 1861-5, while I was a member of Company I. 20th Regt. Mass. Vol. Inf., attached to the third brigade second division Second army Corps. and always with the Army of the Potomac commanded by Gen'ls; Pope, McClellan, Burnside, Hooker, Meade and Grant covering a period of about two years. I enlisted as a Private and rose to the rank of Orderly Sergeant, about the same as having a Lieutenant Commission offered to me if I would reenlist but I did not choose to remain, it was too hard a life for me.

As an appendix I have added a few short stories written from personal observations.

This history was written in the winter of 1895-6.

Josiah F. Murphey

The following I wrote for the Nantucket Journal at the request of the editor Mr. Arthur H. Gardner.[3]

The Battle of Antietam.[4]

When the war broke out I was employed as a clerk in the Union store[5] under Mr. C.H. Bailey[6] and I caught the fever in August, 1862. Being a minor I had to get the consent of my parents and signed the rolls with Mr. F.J. Crosby, in one of the ante rooms of the old Pantheon Hall then used as a recruiting office.[7] After about twenty of us had signed the rolls we bid adieu to family, wives and sweethearts and left for Boston by early steamer. Our coming was telegraphed from Hyannis and when we arrived in Boston a fife and drum met us at the depot and we were marched to headquarters to the tune of the Raw Recruit which ran thus:

> I'm a raw recruit with a bran[d] new suit
> One hundred dollars bounty,
> I'm going down to Washington,
> To fight for Nantucket County.

We stayed in Boston a day or two buying a few needed articles and then went out to Cambridge to Camp Cameron.[8] I should think there were about four or five thousand men there of every nationality and it was a hard place. We really began to see something of the life of a soldier. The camp occupied about forty or fifty acres and had a guard stationed around it to keep the men from getting out. A small brook ran through it where every morning could be seen three or four hundred men with soap and towel performing their morning Toilets.

At the end of about three weeks we were paid thirteen dollars for one month's pay. This was about Aug. 27th, 1862. We went direct to Washington, D.C., and stopped at the Soldiers' Retreat[9] one night and started early on the morning of August 29th, for our regiment, the 20th Mass., Co. I, then encamped about four miles from Alexandria, Va. We crossed Long Bridge soon after sunrise and reached Arlington heights overlooking the city of Washington and it was a beautiful sight. We had a long and tiresome march to reach our regiment and stopped several times to lighten our knapsacks of extras in the shape of clothing. We reached our regiment about four o'clock PM all played out. We met the Nantucket boys who had come out about a year previous and they told us that they were having a hard time marching and fighting.

We thought when we left home that we should have tents to sleep in and the best of medical attendence. We soon found out, however, that, all the tent we should have would be what we could carry, that our bed would be the cold ground and our covering would be whatever blankets we could carry in our knapsacks which consisted of one rubber and one woolen; well we were in for it and were determined to make the best of it.

We remained in camp two or three hours and then started on another march leaving our knapsacks in a pile under guard so as to put ourselves in what was termed light marching order. We marched up to the battlefield of the second Bull Run to help cover the retreat of Gen. Pope[10] I think we marched until about midnight when we halted and when the order came to break ranks I stepped back a few feet from the road, laid down on the ground and was soon fast asleep after one of the hardest marches that it was ever my lot to perform. We were all new men wholly unused to marching and estimating that we had made about thirty miles that day it was certainly a hard one for us and we slept without being rocked. The next morning we were up bright and early and moved to the front and as I said before, helped to cover the retreat from the second Bull Run fight which was a victory for the Rebels.

We remained in camp a few days after the battle and then took up the line of march to South Mountain. We passed through Fredericktown, Md., made famous by Whittier's poem of Barbara Fritchie.[11]

We were held in reserve at the battle of South Mountain, Sept. 14th,[12] until midnight and then marched to the front to relieve the ninth corps under Gen. Reno.[13] It was a toilsome night's march. The roads were filled with ambulances conveying wounded men to the hospital, relieved regiments going to the rear, relieving regiments going to the front ready for the next day's attack, artillery, cavalry, men with stretchers bearing wounded to the rear, and among them two stretcher bearers with the body of Gen. Reno, one of the most promising officers of the Potomac Army who was killed that day. It was at that battle that I saw the first dead Rebs and we cut the buttons from their clothes to send home as mementoes, and it was here most of us got our guns which we picked up on the battlefield[14] It was here that I first saw a rebel officer who came into our lines under a flag of truce (a white cloth tied on a stick) to get the body of some officer who was killed. As we marched along the road we passed several Rebs laying on the sides who had given out and had been left by their men. We spoke to them and asked them what regiment they belonged to and gave them a word of cheer by telling them that our ambulances would shortly be along and take them in and to the hospital, of course as prisoners, but while in the hospital they would be treated the same as our own men. They thanked us and we left them.

The Rebel General Lee[15] had crossed the Potomac into Maryland and had established himself near Antietam Creek and to that place our army directed its course. We arrived at the creek, forded the same and went into line of battle shortly after and moved forward through a field of standing corn over Virginia fences and into an open field where we (the recruits) received our baptismal fire of solid shot, shell, grape and cannister, minnie balls, and every thing else that goes to make up the defence of an enemy. Artillerymen cheered us as we passed as the enemy were being driven back. To us who had been but a few days in the service it was certainly a thrilling time. The ground around us was strewn with everything that pertains to war, dismounted cannon, broken caissons, soldiers guns and knapsacks all thickly intermingled with dead and wounded soldiers of both sides. As we neared the wounded they would raise themselves up and motion us not tread on them. We passed on and entered a piece of wood and became engaged with the enemy. The roar of musketry and artillery, the bursting of shells, the commands of the officers mingled with the shrieks and groans of the wounded, all went to make a scene unequalled anywhere except on the battlefield. Our troops gradually drove the enemy all day and we went into camp that night on the outskirts of the village of Sharpsburg. When morning dawned Sept. 18, our foe had fled leaving his dead and wounded on the field and many prisoners in our hands. I went over a part of the field and many of their dead lay in regular rows just as they had fallen. They would make a stand for a while, fall back and make another and their line of dead showed where each stand had been made. It was a disasterous day for Lee when he crossed into Maryland and he returned [to Virginia] as soon as possible. Our Regimental loss in Antietam was 148. History says that more men were lost in this battle in the same length of time than was lost in any other battle of the war.[16] We encamped for a few days in the vicinity of the battlefield and then started on the march for Harper's Ferry. We reached the Potomac river late one afternoon. We forded the river about two and a half feet deep, and passed through the town and saw the house where John Brown lived, also the engine house where he made a fight for the liberty of the southern slave, passed through the little town of Boliver to the heights beyond where we went into camp for the night.[17] But very little sleep came to us that night. We were on high hills and a cold wind was blowing and with our clothing soaked with the water of the Potomac and not wood enough to keep fire, it was certainly uncomfortable, but such is a soldier's life and it was no use to grumble.[18]

Encamped at Boliver Heights.[19]
REVIEWED BY PRESIDENT LINCOLN.

How We Lived, What We Lived On, and
How it was Furnished Us.

In my previous article published February 23, the *Journal*, makes me say that we were paid twenty-five dollars for one month's pay. It should read thirteen. We were paid thirteen dollars per month, fed, and allowed forty-three dollars per year for clothing.

We remained encamped on Boliver Heights doing picket and other military duty. It was here that I first saw President Lincoln.[Murphey penciled in the following: I saw Lincoln at Boliver heights about Oct or Nov. 1862].[20] He came on from Washington and reviewed the army encamped about here. While here we lived in what is termed shelter tents, which consists of a piece of thin cotton drilling about one and a half yards square with buttons and button holes on three sides. Two pieces are buttoned together to form the roof and two half pieces to form the ends. Three poles are cut, two for the uprights and one for the ridge pole, and the pieces buttoned together and thrown over this forms the roof. The three-cornered end pieces are then buttoned on and the tent is complete. We then dig a trench around the outside to keep the water from coming in on us when we are asleep. We generally pitched on a slight incline so that the water would run away from us. Two of us occupied one tent. The tents were not high enough to stand up in and the entrance was made on all fours. Although rather small they were a luxury which we enjoyed but when it rained very hard the water would come right through and wet us although it was a little better than being outside, and I would mention here that when campaigning in the field without tents we were often awakened in the night by the rain drops striking us in the face. We would pull our heads under the rubber blanket and take another nap but most always awoke in the morning with some parts thoroughly wet, having been exposed to the rain. As we had no change of outer clothing we could do nothing but let them dry when the weather was better. We marched, fought and slept in the rain. When it rained we got wet and when the sun shone we got dry.

While on the subject I may as well tell you how we lived, what we had to eat and how we got it.

The Government allows a plenty of rations to the soldier but the difficulty experienced in getting it to him when in the field often causes him to get short and go very hungry. Our food consisted principally of hard bread and pork, salt and fresh meat, coffee and sugar, and once in a while a little tea. The hard bread was most always good except once in a while there would be a small, dark bug in it which we did not mind so long as we could see them. Our fresh meat was carried right along with us on the hoof and was killed as needed. While on a forced march we lived on hard tack, raw salt pork and coffee for days at a time. Sometimes we would fry the pork in a little tin pan that we always carried, but more often it was eaten raw, with hard tack and coffee.

Our food was carried in covered teams drawn by six mules and was issued to the Quartermaster who in turn issued it to a sergeant of each company and he to the men. Once in a while the Johnnies would make a raid upon our teams and capture a large number with our rations. We would then be cut short until some more could be furnished. Each brigade or regiment would take turns in guarding our ration teams while on the march. Once while we were guarding the wagon train, it was eleven miles long which will give some idea of the amount of food it took to take care of us, We carried our own food in what is called a haversack which is simply a cotton bag about 12 or 18 inches square with a coating of rubber to keep the water out and a strap to go over the shoulders to carry it by. Our tin plate was carried in this and I always used mine for a pillow at night; rather hard, but then I soon got used to it and slept just as sound as though it were feathers. Our water was carried in a round, flat ves-

sel, called a canteen, holding about three pints. Our water was
obtained from springs, ponds, rivers and when we were very thirsty
we did not scruple to drink out of the puddles in the road. I have
drank water from holes made by the horses' hoofs and filled with
rain. Now don't say "Oh!" because you would have done the same
thing if you had been without water as long as I had. I always tried
to have water in my canteen when going into battle because if I was
wounded and could not get off the field I knew the service water
would be to me. Another thing I always looked out for and that was
to have an old letter with the envelope always somewhere about me
so that if killed in battle my friends might know what became of
me. Thousands of headstones in the National Cemeteries bear the
single word "Unknown" which might have been different had some
such plan as mine been adopted.

I have often been asked if I was not scared when going into battle.
Well, I cannot say that I ever had what you might call real fright.
When going into battle the excitement and the fact that we are bound
to obey orders under the penalty of death, and the idea of being called
a coward in the face of the enemy takes all else from your mind but
the thought of beating them and cowardice in battle was a very rare
thing, and I never knew of but very few cases with us. Getting
inside the line of where the solid shot (cannon balls) and shell are
falling and bursting was always the most dreaded part of a battle to
me. Once inside that line then you only have the musket balls to fear,
(which of course are enough), but as I say once inside that line and
then you load and fire as rapidly as possible, paying no attention to
the enemy's bullets. A cry from some comrade close to you will cause
you to turn in time to see some one of your company fall either killed
or wounded. The space is immediately closed up and you go on in
your harvest of death, If the wounded can manage to crawl off why
they do so but with our regiment we were not allowed to leave the
line while the battle was going on. There is one more thing that a
soldier dreads while in a battle and that is grape and canister which
is always used when both lines are at short range or close together.

It is round and about an inch in diameter, made of iron. They differ in size somewhat and are made up in cases and put into the cannon and fired with the same effect as a charge of shot from a hunter's gun, scattering and making a big gape in an advancing line, whistling all sorts of tunes and frequently taking off ten or twelve men, killed and wounded at one discharge. Bursting shells and grape and canister are the missles that the soldier most dreads as both will tear the flesh in a most horrid manner.

A line of battle consists of two lines of men, one in front of the other, called front and rear rank and in this way advance with colors a few steps in front of the line solidly up to the enemy's position. A line of battle will be anywhere from one half to two miles in length and sometimes even more. The centre of the regiment is where the colors are and the color guard consists of five corporals and a sergeant and I do not think that I ever went into a battle but what the color sergeant was either killed or wounded. He makes a good target and we all aim to bring down the colors but for all that I never saw the time when men were wanted who were not all ready to take the colors and when they fell in battle there were always plenty to rush and pick them up knowing at the time that they were almost sure to be shot in so doing. A battery consists generally of twelve cannon with caisson which carry the shot and shell and is placed in battle to the rear of the front line. The cannon are elevated so as to fire over our heads into the enemy's line. A high position is chosen if possible which gives great advantage.

A skirmish line is a line of men about twenty feet apart singly and always [in] advance about fifty or a hundred feet in front of the regular line of battle so as to feel the enemy and draw their fire that we may know where they are and how many they consist of. If a man ever thinks he is made a special target of he will think so when on the skirmish line as just as soon as he begins to drive their pickets they will begin to fire and when you see them bring their gun up and take deliberate aim at you before they fall back you will certainly think that you are going to get hit. When you have drawn the fire of their line of battle you fall back on your own line and advance with it and the battle becomes general. Another of the dreaded things of the Union soldier life was the thought of being taken prisoner. Many men of our regiment had been taken prisoners and the stories they told us of their hardships made us vow that we would run some hard risks before we would consent to go to Richmond. Of the horrors of Libby[21] and Andersonville[22] I cannot tell as I was fortunate enough never to be taken prisoner but from those who were some terrible tales are told and I believe them as they all tell the same story.

In my next I will take up my story where I left off in my former letter when we crossed the Potomac and encamped at Boliver Heights.

At Fredericksburg[23]

From our camp at Boliver Heights, near Harper's Ferry, we could look about twenty miles into the country and see the main body of the rebs. We went on picket about two miles out into the country and frequently while on duty a rebel deserter would come into our lines, having got tired of service on that side.

The railroad bridge at Harper's Ferry had been destroyed and the engine and cars run off the end and lay piled one on top of the other in the river. The U.S. Arsenal building had also been destroyed. It looked wicked to see such wanton destruction of property. While here a raid was made to Charleston, Va. which was about fifteen miles away.[24] The rebel guard was surprised and twenty thousand bushels of grain were destroyed by our troops. We left this camp about November 1, 1862, crossed the Shenandoah River on a pontoon bridge and marched through a pleasant valley where we feasted on many kinds of fruit, and made our next camp at the small village of Warrington. While here the troops were drawn up in line on the side of the road to bid farewell to their beloved commander, General George B. McClellan,[25] the army having been put in command of General Ambrose E. Burnside.[26] We cheered and fired salutes to our late commanding officer for we were all very much attached to him, but the great powers in Washington saw fit to remove him so he must go, and while General Burnside made a very good corps commander he was not fit to command an army as the sequel proved. We passed on from Warrington to the banks of the Rappahannock at Fredericksburg where the rebs disputed our passage. We were camped about three fourths of a mile from the river back of a small town called Falmouth and would frequently make a trip to the river to see what the rebs were doing on the other side. We could see that they were building strong lines of works.

The country back of Fredericksburg rises to quite a height and the hills are called Marye's Heights. On these heights the rebs built their lines of works three or four of them, one overlooking the other like seats in a theatre, only farther apart. Each line could get in its work by firing over the heads of those in front, a little risky, perhaps, but then they take risks in battle. The rebs also built a line of breastworks in front of the city next to the river where they were to make their first resistance.

We remained in this camp about three weeks and while here we built log huts about eight feet square and covered them with tenting. We got stones and built a fireplace, plastering them with clay mud and topping up with sticks of wood and lining the whole with clay. We foraged about the country and collected boards enough to build bunks and were just beginning to take things comfortable when we had to pack up and move.

On the eleventh day of December, 1862, we were out on picket, I myself being on the reserve with others. It was about three in the morning and I had just left the fire to get a little sleep, when I was roused by the order to fall in. Men were sent to the outposts to call in those who were there and from the fact that no relief was put on in their place we knew that something was up. We fell in and marched back to camp distant about a mile or so and were ordered to break ranks, pack up and be ready to move in about an hour. When we got into our quarters, (the log huts before mentioned) we sat down and talked the matter over. Well we knew what was in store for us, we knew that we were to make an attempt to cross the river and gain the city and take the heights beyond, and knowing how strongly fortified the rebs were we knew what a reception we should get, and that many of us would never see the light of another day. However we were soldiers and must take our chances. About daylight the drum beat to fall in and we fell in. After we had formed in line ready to march, our commanding officer asked one of the men of our company if he would volunteer as one of the color guard. He immediately did so, but at the same time made this remark, "Good-bye boys, you will never see me again," expecting to be killed, as it is the most exposed place in the regiment. Well he was not killed, but so badly wounded that he never returned to the regiment and we never did see him again.

About sunrise the signal gun was fired and we started for the scene of what was to be one of the hardest fought battles of the war. We reached the river in about half an hour. The city was enveloped in a fog; the 50th N.Y. Engineers had the pontoon bridge about one third done and the rebs would not let them lay another plank.[27] Everything was at a standstill. Franklin's troops[28] could be seen way down the river crossing on a pontoon bridge, and here let me describe a pontoon bridge: It is a floating bridge made of square end boats that we would term scows, anchored at both ends, headed up and down stream about 10 or 15 feet apart. Timbers fitted for the purpose are placed across them from boat to boat and planking laid across the timber and another set of timber laid over the planking to keep them in place. It makes a good bridge over which artillery, infantry and cavalry can pass in safety.

Our trouble now was to get a bridge across the river to which the rebs objected very decidedly. All along our side of the river on a high bluff, was posted cannon, about 150 pieces in all, extending the whole front of the city lines. When the engineers attempted to continue building the bridge the rebs would open fire on them at close range.[29] They [the Engineers] were not able to return the fire as they were unarmed and could not live under it. This would be the signal for the artillery to open fire, and beginning on the right the whole 150 pieces would hurl their iron missles of death into the doomed city. It was a grand but a terrible sight. The church steeples were pierced through and through, chimneys were thrown down, solid shot would crash through the private dwellings, both wooden and brick, and the city was fired in several places. Standing near a cannon you could range it and tell about where the shot would strike and when it was fired, splinters, bricks and mortar would tell how true the aim of the gunner had been. But it was impossible to depress the guns enough to drive out the rebel sharpshooters from near the bank of the river.

This kind of work continued at intervals throughout the whole day and we were no nearer crossing than in the morning and something had to be done. Burnside called for volunteers to charge over in pontoon boats and drive the rebel sharpshooters from the bank of the river and our brigade commander [Colonel Norman Hall][30] offered the services of our brigade. Col. Hall said, "my soldiers are ready to cross the river in the boats and drive out the Confederates." Permission was granted and it was planned that the boats would be ready on the shore and the troops at a given signal should rush down to the bank of the river, jump into the boats and pull quickly across, [and] charge up the bank on the other side. It was a desperate game and the poet Boker[31] thus pictures the scene:

> They leaped into the rocking shallops,
>   Ten offered where one could go,
> And the breeze was alive with laughter
>   Till the boatman began to row.
>
> "How many? I judge four hundred;"
> "Who are they? I know to a man;"
> Our own Nineteenth and Twentieth,
>   And the Seventh Michigan.

Then the shore where the rebels harbored,
Was fringed with a gush of flame,
And buzzing like bees o'er the water
The swarms of their bullets came.

In silence, how dread and solemn!
With courage, how grand and true!
Steadily, steadily onward
The line of shallops drew.

Not a whisper! Each man was conscious
He stood in sight of death!
So he bowed to the awful presence,
And treasured his living breath,

'Twixt death in the air above them
And death in the waves below,
Through balls and grape and shrapnell
They neared—my God! how slow!

And many a brave stout fellow,
Who sprang in the boats with mirth,
Ere they made that fatal crossing
Was a load of lifeless earth.

And many a brave stout fellow,
Whose limbs with strength were rife,
Was torn and crushed and shattered—
A helpless wreck for life.

Cheer after cheer we sent them,
As only armies can,
Cheer for old Massachusetts!
Cheers for young Michigan!

They formed a line of battle,
Not a man was out of place!
Then with level steel they hurled them,
Straight in the rebel's face.

And thus they crossed the river,
Hear me, man, from rear to van;
Three cheers for old Massachusetts!
And three more for young Michigan.

After getting into the boat two men sat down at the oars; one was Thomas Russell[32] of this town, the other man I do not remember, but he pulled Russell right around and headed the boat upstream. Lieut. Leander F. Alley[33] said to me, "Murphey, take that oar," which I did and we soon had the boat across on the other side where she grounded a few feet from the shore. We jumped out and waded to the land. The other boats [containing the Seventh Michigan and Nineteenth Mass.] had got there first, had charged up the bank, [and had] driven out the rebel sharpshooters and taken with the wounded about twenty [Confederate] prisoners, who were brought back in the first boats that returned after we got across and before the pontoon bridge was finished. But now that the sharpshooters were driven away from the bank our engineers soon had the bridge completed and the troops in reserve were beginning to move across it. We lay under the bank of the city and as soon as the troops began to cross we were ordered forward. Our company formed in two platoons of about thirty men each at the lowest end of a street called Farquier street[34] and began our advance up the street. As soon as we came in sight of the rebels who were concealed in every house and behind every fence they opened a terrible fire on us at short range and our men began dropping at every point, those struck in the vital parts dropping without a sound, but those wounded otherwise would cry out with pain as they fell or limped to the rear. But despite the terrible fire we pressed on up the street. Where men fell and left a vacant place other men stepped into their places and although death stared us in the face there was not a man who faltered. Our chief company officer Capt. H.L. Abbott[35] said "hold your fire, boys, until you see something to fire at."

We had now arrived at the corner of a cross street called Caroline street[36] and I, being on the left flank of the company, turned to look down the street to see if anything could be seen to fire at and bringing my gun to the ready at the same time. At that moment I felt a sharp stinging pain on the right side of my face and presto, I knew no more.

When I came to I was lying on the ground where I had fallen, and the company had advanced a short distance up the street. The balls were still flying thick around me and I realized I was wounded. I clapped my hand to my face to stop the flow of blood but it was no use. It flowed between my fingers and down onto my clothing and

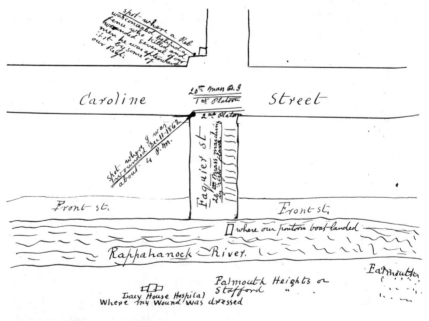

Josiah F. Murphey's hand-drawn map of the streets of Fredericksburg, where he was wounded.

filled me full. I got up rather faint, and a feeling of madness came over me, and a word in your ear gentle reader and let it go no further, I swore; I cursed the whole southern confederacy from Virginia to the gulf of Mexico; but on a second thought I realized it was war and banished such thoughts from my mind and made my way across the river to a hospital called the Lacy house,[37] so named from its former occupants. When I got there it was about one third full. A nurse came along and said he would take a few stitches in my wound for me. He went off to get his needle and I never saw him afterwards. Men were coming in so thick that he was probably called to more serious cases.

But return with me a few minutes to the regiment still advancing up the street. They drove the rebels out from their concealment, but at a terrible loss of life. Think of it, a company of about sixty men advancing up a street with no protection whatever and two or three hundred of the enemy sheltered completely and pouring a murderous fire upon upon you from every window, door, and behind every fence. They would even poke their guns around the corner of the houses and fire into us at close range. (Let me here put in what Walker in his history of the Second Corps says with reference to the part our regiment took in cleaning the streets):

> The Twentieth Mass. is called upon to clear the streets which lead from the bridge-head up through the city. It is a perilous task: the enemy's fire sweeps straight down to the water. But never was a better regiment called to the perilous task than the Twentieth Massachusetts.
>
> "I cannot," says Colonel Hall, "presume to express all that is due the officers and men of this regiment, for the unflinching bravery and splendid discipline shown in the execution of this order. Platoon after platoon was swept away, but the head of the column did not falter. Ninety seven officers and men were killed or wounded in the space of about fifty yards.[38]

We lost about forty men from our company in the space of fifty yards. In no battle of the war in which we were afterwards engaged did we lose so many men in so short a time.[39] But reinforcements arrived and the rebs were finally driven entirely out of the city and our boys occupied the houses and regaled themselves while they stayed.

The most of the inhabitants left before the fight began and our troops occupied the houses, broke open the stores and helped themselves to whatever pleased their fancy most.

Let us make a comparison. Nantucket occupies about the same area that Fredericksburg does, but the latter has more inhabitants. Now, suppose an army was about to bombard the town. The inhabitants would naturally leave in a hurry, taking but very little with them, and when the hostile troops gained the town what a picnic would be in store for them. They would enter the houses and stores and help themselves. Well, that is just the state in which we found Fredericksburg when we entered the city, and of course the troops considered it common property and took whatever they wanted.

In this battle Nantucket lost more of her sons than in any other one battle of the war.[40] I have a list of the killed and wounded from this town.

In the hospital where I was men were constantly arriving, wounded in all parts of the body and I thought best to secure a place to sleep for the night. I chose a place near the chimney in the corner of the room. There were no beds and each one made himself as comfortable as he could on the floor. On one side of me laid a rebel from the 13th Mississippi regiment.[41] He was a bright fellow and I talked with him many hours about the war and its causes. When I told him to what regiment I belonged he said: "I have met your regiment three times in battle," and when I asked him how he knew he said, "Once at Balls Bluff,[42] and we beat you there." I said yes, and he continued, "We fought you at Fair Oaks,"[43] and I said, "We beat you there." He said "Yes, I was wounded and taken prisoner," and strange to say he was wounded and taken prisoner here at Fredericksburg and both times wounded in the hip. This man told me he thought Massachusetts and South Carolina ought to fight the war out. About an hour after I was wounded a Nantucket man of our company was brought in on a stretcher, suffering terribly from a wound and crying out with pain. As soon as he caught sight of me he begged me piteously to kill him and end his sufferings. I spoke to him and told him that the attendant would help him in a few minutes and in a short time one appeared and gave him something that quieted him and he went to sleep. He did not wake again until the next morning and then his pain had left him. I asked him if he wanted I should fulfil his request of the night before and he said "No, but I was in such pain I did not care what became of me." He is living today, has a family and has been a carrier in the Boston postoffice for a number of years.[44] Of course there was no sleep for us that night except for those under the influence of opiates. The hospital we were in was a large brick mansion and it was filled to overflowing, many wounded lying on the ground outside but as they died inside they were removed and those outside were taken in. Think of it, wounded and unable to help yourself, and lying on the ground in the month of December with only a rubber blanket between you and the cold earth; but it could not be helped. As soon as possible the wounded were taken on the cars to Acquia creek landing,[45] and thence on the steamer to Washington.

The next day, Friday, was occupied mostly by our commanding officer, Gen. Burnside, in getting troops across the river and placing them in position to make a charge. The next day our regiment occupied the extreme right of the line. Saturday morning, Dec. 13, the grand charge was made on the rebel lines of works but they were too strong for our side and for hours the fighting continued with the balance strongly on the side of the rebels. Regiment after regiment was put into the fight and brigade after brigade only to be driven back with terrible slaughter. Gen. Burnside was besought to withdraw his troops, but he continued fighting all day until darkness closed the contest. It was his intention to renew the fight in the morning but he thought better of it and the next day, Sunday, was passed in comparative quiet as well as Monday, but Monday evening our troops began to recross the river, the wounded having previously been sent over and by morning of the sixteenth were about all over and the battle of Fredericksburg, one of the bloodiest battles of the war, passed into history as a defeat for the Union army. It did seem like sheer barbarism to hurl troops against those three lines of breastworks arranged as they were so one could fire over the heads of those in the lines in front of him and the rebs themselves say that the advantage was all on their side. They lost but a very few men compared to us.[46]

While lying in the hospital on the 13th during the battle, a rebel solid shot struck it and made it tremble all over. It did no damage as far as I know but we held our breath expecting every minute another would come tearing through the walls and perhaps into the room where we were lying, but none others struck us.

While our regiment was in the fight of the 13th, Lieut. Leander F. Alley of this town was killed. The ball entered his left eye and lodged in the brain. After he fell our regiment fell back and Capt. Abbott perceiving that Alley was killed and left some distance in front of our line, called for volunteers to bring off his body and four or five of our company, mostly Nantucket men, crawled up under a heavy fire and brought off the body. It was placed in charge of Lieut. John W. Summerhays who in turn placed it in my charge to bring home, he having procured me a furlough for that purpose, and after preparing the body as well as possible under the circumstances I left for Washington via Acquia creek and from thence to Boston and Nantucket where services were held in the North Congregational church of which many of our present prominent citizens attended.[47] I wish before I close this to say a few more words about an army hospital, or what is more properly termed a field hospital. It is a tent, a house, a barn or a shed, and often simply the shelter given by some large tree. If it be a tent, or a building, the wounded are brought in and put into it until it is crowded and then the rest are laid on the rubber blankets of the soldiers on the ground and in that way cared for until transportation is furnished them to Washington or some other place where comfortable quarters are assigned them and are kindly cared for. If at these hospitals it was their good fortune to come under the care of the Sanitary Commission, the Christian Commission[48] or any of the female nurses, and most every hospital had some one of these, then it was that they received the kindest of care and thousands upon thousands of soldiers owe their lives to the untiring care given them by the ladies working in these hospitals.

I had often heard the men in our company who, when wounded, had been in the hospital and afterwards returned to the regiment, speak of the horrors of a field hospital and it was even so. Men lay in the room where I was, wounded in almost every part of the body, some only with flesh wounds like mine, others terribly torn and mangled and in awful pain, but after the first few hours there was scarcely a sound from them. All seemed to realize that their neighbor had as bad a wound as they had and each tried his best to keep quiet.In the room next to ours the surgeons were busy amputating, and the arms and legs of the unfortunate ones were thrown in a pile out of doors, and after the horrible work was all done, buried at one time, and should I ever visit the Lacy house (which is still standing) I think I could point out the spot where many a northern soldier left part of his body in the south.

Of the six or eight Nantucket boys[49] who gave their lives for their country in this battle, I would say a few words in favor of one of them, Lieut. Leander F. Alley. He rose from the ranks as a private to the office of second lieutenant and was such when a rebel bullet found the fatal spot. He was an officer much beloved by every man in the regiment and it was a sad loss to us when he was killed. Never rash but always brave he was ever looking to the interests of those under his charge.

With us was a father and his son who fought side by side, and when, on the thirteenth day of December, Burnside made his famous charge this father and son went forward in our line of battle to do their part. They had not advanced far when a bullet from a rebel gun laid the father low in death. It was more than the boy could stand and he left the ranks without permission and was arrested and tried by a court-martial. At the trial he told why he left the ranks. He could stand almost anything but to see his father shot dead by his side was more than his nature could endure.When the story was told he was immediately discharged and afterwards served with honor. No one could

blame him. Which of us could stand such a trial and not falter?[50]
The battle of Fredericksburg was a disastrous blow to the Union army
and twelve thousand were killed and wounded. The Confederates
lost only about one half as many.

In connection with this story I will add a short poem written by
Mrs. P. A. Hanaford[51] on the death of Lieut. Alley at the time.

> Brave and true-hearted; in his country's cause,
>   His life he hath lain down;
> Noble the deed, and History's page shall tell,
>   He wore a martyr's crown.
>
> Aye, woven with the amaranthine flowers.
>   Which bloom where angels dwell,
> While patriots' hearts beside his grave may plant,
>   In love the asphodel.
>
> God comfort those who mourn his early loss,
>   And wipe their tears away,
> With thoughts of meeting him again at last.
>   Where beams th' eternal day.
>
> Where warlike deeds, for aye are known no more,
>   And peace rules in each heart,
> And sainted heroes loving friends shall greet
>   No more—oh, joy!—to part.
>
> Beneath the green sods of his native isle,
>   His honored dust shall rest—
> His memory liveth, as a patriot true,
>   In many a grateful breast.
>
> Write now the name of Alley on thy list,
>   Oh Fame! and write it high:—
> Nantucket's brave, heroic sons may fall,
>   Their names shall never die.

SECTION TWO

After attending the last sad rites of the burial of Lieut. Alley's body
I returned to Boston and my ten days furlough having expired and
my wound not being healed I called on Col. Day,[1] then commanding troops around Boston and he extended my furlough. Lieut. Wm
R. Riddle[2] of our Regt. who had lost an arm had me detailed to stay
in his recruiting office on Portland street until my wound would allow
me to return to my Regiment. In the mean time I made two or
three trips to Nantucket.

I finally returned to my regiment which was located at Falmouth
Va. just above the city of Fredericksburg on the opposite side of the
river (Rappahanock) only a short distance from where we were
encamped when we went into the battle. I found our regiment occupying negro or slave quarters with nice wooden bunks to sleep in
doing picket duty on the river front. This was in march 1863.

While here we fared well catching fish in the river and having a good
many other dainties which we could not get when encamped in the
woods. While in this camp we used to buy pies of a poor widow who
lived opposite at 25 cents a piece about six inches across and with
not a particle of shortening in them, it could not be procured. Flour
was thirty dollars a barrell and had to be hauled eight or ten miles.

We remained in Falmouth until about the first of May of same
year (1863) when we again crossed the river and took part in the
Battle of Chancellorsville.[3] About the last of April 1863 [we] were
given eight days rations and ordered to hold ourselves in readiness
to march at any moment.

May 2nd we moved down and across the river [Rappahannock] on
a pontoon bridge and without much opposition entered the city of
Fredericksburg, passing over about the same ground on which we
fought so hard in the December previous. But now, the Rebs had
left the city. It showed the marks of the former struggle, scarcely a
house but had a hole in it made during the bombardment of Dec.
11th 12th 13th 1862. Some were patched up with boards and some

with pieces of sheet iron to keep out the weather. Others were left just as when the battle ended. Many of the citizens were still in the city to protect as far as possible their homes.

We passed through the city and on the heights beyond we found the Rebs posted, with artillery and troops to dispute our passage. We were first to the front on the skirmish line and prepared to charge but found upon advancing that in between us and the Rebs. was a canal about ten feet wide and as many deep, which stopped our advance. The troops on our left that held the road charged up the hill and drove the Rebs from the works capturing two pieces of artillery from the famos Washington artillery of New Orleans[4] and a few prisoners. We occupied the heights [Marye's] we tried so hard to capture the December previous. We slept in the streets of the city that night. After we got back into the city in the afternoon and had stacked our guns we took a stroll around to see what was to be seen. Houses and contents had been badly shattered, holes through their sides large enough to crawl through and the furniture smashed.

In one house we visited on the outskirts where one side was open to the force of the bullets fired from Marye's Heights by the enemy at our line of battle on Dec 13-1862. It was completely riddled looking like the holes in a pepper box, a large hole showed where a shell had come through the side of the house, bursted in the room and two pieces [of the shell] lay on top of the piano. The windows of the room were broken, plastering knocked down, and everything in general disorder. Such was war, cruel resistless war.

After driving the Rebs from Mary's heights May 2 we left troops to hold the enemy in check, and our regiment returned to the city and stacked our guns on the north side of the street where the freight depot is located. I remember the night well it was a beautiful moonlight night and as I laid down to sleep on the earth sidewalk with the grass that [had] grown close to the fence for a pillow, I got to thinking of my home way up north in old Nantucket and as I gazed at the bright clear moon I wondered if any of my friends at home were at that moment looking at the same moon and while musing thus I fell asleep to dream (as I often did) of that far away home, dreamed that I was there enjoying their pleasures and their comforts, but was awakened from that dream by the shrill call of the bugle sounding the Reveille, and learned that we were to go to the front and take our turn on the picket line. Later in the day we could see that the Rebs were filling up the breastworks we had driven them out of up on the hills and I learned that our troops on our immediate right had been unsuccessful and that we were likely to be attacked.

That night May 2-1863 I could from my post on the picket line hear the Rebs talking plainly through the fog and we kept close watch as we expected the rebs would charge our lines at daylight. I was relieved from my post on picket about two o'clock in the morning and went back into the city and slept with the rest of our company. When morning came there was a dense fog and under cover of that we called in our picket line and fell back across the river, and swung our pontoon bridge over the whole.

We returned to our old camp at Falmouth and thus ended the part we took in the battle of Chancellorsville, the second attempt to capture and Fredericksburg had failed.

In the latter part of June 1863 we left our quarters at Falmouth Va. and with the rest of the army started to head off the Rebs. who had gone on a raid into Penn.[5] We had some terrible forced marching, often thirty miles a day, and were kept at it through mud and rain. I took a severe cold by having to sleep in wet clothes and was ordered to the hospital. The ambulance took us about 20 or 30 of us 5 or six miles to a train and we started for Alexandria Va. after halting once or twice for the guard on the train to drive back Rebel Cavalry. We reached Alexandria about 9 P.M. and were taken in ambulances and carried to the Hospital which was located on Washington st opposite the library building. It was a Baptist Church converted into a Hospital.[6] I remained here for about 6 or eight weeks sick and recovering from an attack of Typhoid fever. I returned to my Regt. about Oct-1863. While in the Hospital I witnessed several operations. I saw one or two arms and legs amputated [and] I also saw a man's skull cut open after he has passed away, one quarter of it taken off and the brain taken out. This was done to determine the location of a minnie ball that had entered just behind the ear, from which wound the man survived eight days. The ball was found at the base of the brain. When I returned to the front I found our Regt. encamped on the Orange and Alexandria R. Road about sixty miles from Alexandria at a place called Brandy Station near Mine Run.[7] December 7th 1863. We started on a march and crossed the Rapidann river, had a skirmish with the enemy and returned to camp, being absent about two days and nights.[8] The mud on this march was terrible. It was cold enough to freeze and our passing over the clay roads after they had begun to thaw, with Artillery and supply wagons made the mud like morter and it was like stepping into a morter bed about one foot deep and then you would bring up on the solid clay beneath.

We would stumble and fall down and our rifle's would go entirely out of sight. We were a hard looking set when we arrived back in camp. We were under fire two or three times in this skirmish but lost no men, the firing being at long range, principally with artillery. We returned to camp and continued our regular routine duty of Picket, Camp Guard drills & etc. Nothing more disturbed us during the winter. Our winter quarters were square log huts with cotton tenting for roof, a stone fireplace and wooden chimney lined with clay mud, and although it was pretty cold sometimes we managed to keep quite comfortable. We remained in camp until May 1864 when we broke camp for another campaign and started about May 2nd 1864[9] for a campaign under General Grant,[10] our corps having been recruited for special service to forty thousand men, under Genl. W.S. Hancock.[11] I will now copy from my diary [in] which I kept adding such events as I can remember.

May 3d 1864. Left camp and marched all night, and the next day crossed the Rapidan at Ely's ford.[12] May 4th. Encamped and rested.

Thursday May 5th. Left camp in the morning and was soon under fire. This was the beginning of the Battle of the Wilderness. We built works and rested for the night.

Friday May 6th. Our company went out on the skirmish line and were out nearly all day and were engaged with the rest of the troops in the heaviest of the Battle in which our Regiment lost heavily.[13] The enemy set the underbrush on fire and charged on us under cover of the smoke, filing out one side when very near us. But we were on the lookout and too quick for them and compelled them under our murderous fire to lie down. We kept our firing on them where they lay and finally compelled them to retreat.

The fire that the enemy set communicated with our breastworks which were built of dead trees and earth. We had to let it burn until the rebs retreated. We then pulled down the works each side of the fire and built around it, letting the fire burn itself out.

In this battle our color sargeant, a man named Fuches,[14] was wounded and the colors fell to the ground. Two of our regt. ran for them and both seized them at the same time and neither wanted to give them up and fell into a dispute as to which had the best right to them. While thus disputing, a minnie ball came and cut the staff in two between them, which settled the question. It was some time before we were able to replace the staff.

Saturday May 7. We layed behind our works all day expecting another attack but the rebs did not come. We were under fire and skirmishing all day.

Sunday May 8th. We still remained in the breastworks. Genl. Grant with body guard passed us last evening and of course we all cheered him. [But] the rebs, thinking we were making a charge, fired at us but no one was hit. Genl. Meade[15] was with him. After thay passed, the cavalry began to go by and when I retired about nine P.M they were still passing and when I got up in the morning about six they were still going by and continued so the most of the day. After they had got by we took up the line of march and marched to a place called Todds Tavern[16] where we had a sharp skirmish with the enemy in connection with the cavalry, after which we again took up the line of march towards Spottsylvania Court House[17] and encamped on the road for the night.

Monday May 9-1864. Marched and built breastworks three different times to day thinking the rebs were going to attack us, but
they did not. But towards night we crossed the Po river and formed
in line of battle in some thick woods to hold the rebs in check.

Tuesday May 10 1864. Our company went out on the picket line
and the rest of the Regt. were ordered back across the river Po. By
some mistake we were left on the picket line while the rest of our
troops retired across the river. The rebs came down upon us in large
numbers and we fell back only to find that we were unsupported and
we made our way to the river and found the bridge destroyed but
finally managed to get across on the sleepers with the loss of but a
few men. It was a close shave for us as the rebels had already appeared
on our flank.

Tuesday May 11. Moved to the front and built breastworks but
left them about 9 P.M. and started on a march by the left flank. We
were ordered to keep very quiet. We had a very hard march. It was
pitch dark and we marched all night. Just as the day broke of May
12th, say about 4 o'clock, we left the road and marched into a large
field which was filled with soldiers sleeping on their arms who had
arrived earlier in the night. We passed them and formed in line of
battle. It was now broad daylight and we moved forward on a charge.
We surprised the enemy and captured their first line of works and
several thousand prisoners, seventeen stand of colors, twenty-two
pieces of artillery and two Major Generals named Edward Johnson[18]
and Geo. H. Stewart.[19] After fighting for several hours, our regiment were ordered to the rear for a rest. In the excitement and noise
of the battle I with several others of our company did not hear the
order to go to the rear and the regiment marched off without our
knowing it. After a few minutes I discovered they had gone but did
not know where so [I] kept wandering about the battlefield to find
them, all the time under fire, thinking they had been ordered to
another part of the field. While looking for my regiment I was asked
by a captain of a N.Y. regiment[20] to help them resist a charge that
the enemy were preparing to make and I did so. The enemy soon

appeared. We did not wait for them to come up to us but ran forward on a charge to meet them. There were not many of them, and they broke and ran, and we halted. In this skirmish the color sargeant of this New York regiment ran up on top of a little mound with his colors. He was instantly wounded and pitched headlong to the ground, I was quite near him and ran for the colors but a member of his own regiment got there first. While I knew it was almost sure death to pick up those colors, I could not stand by and see them on the ground. What became of the wounded sargeant I do not know as I immediately went forward with the rest. It would of been a little singular for me of a Mass. regt. to of carried to my regiment a New York regiment's colors. In a short time the enemy broke and ran and I continued the search of my regiment all the while under fire as the battle was still going on. From our position in this battle I could look directly into the mouth of two cannon that were directly behind us and firing over our heads, and see every shot that came out of the muzzle. They looked just like a bird darting through the air. It was on this field that the Confederate sword was captured that I have in my possession. But *I* did not capture it.

Some time after noon I perceived our regiment marching across the field and on inquirey I found that they had been to the rear to rest while I had been on the field all day long looking for them. I fell in with them and we marched to another part of the field and again became engaged in the hottest of the fight.[21]

We had in our regiment a young man named Wm P. Kelley son of Doctor J. R. Kelley of Nantucket who was taken prisoner in this battle.[22] The enemy threw up a flag of truce from behind their breastworks and we stopped firing and Kelley with the rest of us went up to the breast works to take them prisoners and he with one or two others were on the top of the works when it was discovered that a traverse divided the enemy inside the works and only one half of them had surrendered. The other half immediately began firing and Kelly with the rest who were on the breastworks had to jump down inside to save their lives. They were taken prisoners and Kelley died in prison. We that were on the ground beat a hasty retreat back to our line of battle, and the fighting went on as usual which had now been raging since daylight, and I had been under fire all the time with nothing to eat except a piece of hard tack snatched from my haversack during an occasional lull in the battle.

Soon after dark we were relieved and went down a short ways into a valley or hollow where all the shot and shell passed over us. We were ordered not to leave the ranks and [to] sleep on our arms. Other troops continued the battle. We laid down on the wet ground (it had been raining all day) and I was asleep in about two minutes and I guess the rest were [too]. We were completely used up from marching all night the night before and fighting all day. I should think I had been asleep about an hour or more when I was awakened by the order to fall in and overheard two officers talking and from what they said I judged the following was the case: our troops in our immediate front were short of ammunition. We had plenty as it had been brought up to us on pack mules while we were in battle. The troops were expecting to be relieved and re-enforcements were already on the way but we were wanted to hold the ground until the reinforcements arrived. We fell into line to again take part in the battle but just as we were about to start the reinforcements arrived and we laid down and were soon again in the arms of Morpheus. The relief were soon hotly engaged as we could tell by the increased firing but I was soon asleep again with the roar of musketry as my lullaby. When I again awoke all was still and the battle was over. We learned that the rebs fell back about midnight to another line of works and the battle of Spottsylvania in which I was under fire for seventeen continuous hours was over. We had driven the rebs from their first line of works, taken many prisoners &c, as I have before stated but we could not dislodge them from their second line of works. I took a short stroll over the battlefield after I had cooked my coffee and had my breakfast which consisted of making a tin of coffee and eating hard tack and salt pork raw. We had nothing else to eat three times a day day after day for several weeks, with occassionally fresh

meat. We ate our pork raw as it made it very salt to fry it. The battlefield was a sight few care to see. The ground was strewn with all
sorts of war material, rifles, cannons, caissons, broken, twisted and
disabled, men and horses lay thick on the ground, wounded, dead,
and dying, it was a terrible sight, but such as we see on all large battlefields. The work of caring for the dead and wounded was rapidly
going on by those detailed to do such work while we (May 13) were
again marched to the left and front and put out on the skirmish line.
Directly in our front were two steel rifled cannon belonging to the
rebs between the lines. They would not let us take them away and
we would not allow them to drag them off. A plan was formed on
our side to suddenly charge and capture the guns. Some troops
were brought up to help us and we formed for the charge. We pressed
as far to the front as possible by crawling on the ground without
attracting any attention from the rebs at a given signal [and] we dashed
forward and before the rebs knew it we had the cannon and were
dragging them in by hand into our lines and to the rear. Some of our
men were wounded but I do not think any were killed.

We remained on the skirmish line all day of the 13th and nearly
all of the 14th but towards night we were relieved and went to the
rear and encamped. We lost 14 men on the skirmish line on the
13th & 14th.

May 15th. Moved to the Fredericksburg plank road and went into
camp.[23] About this time while on picket on the Railroad leading to
Fredericksburg, just before night we saw a squad of Rebs cross the
R.R. and we fired into them as they passed and thought no more of
it. After dark I was on vidette picket on this R.R. and pretty soon I
heard a sound as of a man in pain. I listened and the sound came nearer as though he was wounded and the pain was from his walking. I
reported to the officer in charge and he said stop him when he gets
near enough [The man] kept coming and when near enough, I said,
"Who comes there?" He said, "A friend without the countersign," and
[he] told me he was a wounded man from the 39th Georgia Regt,[24]
that he had no gun and had got turned around and did not know

where he was. I told him he was a prisoner and that our Regt. was the 20th Mass, and he replied, "All right, I cannot help it." He had a slight wound in the ancle and said he was one of the relief picket[s] who had crossed the Railroad just before dark and was hit by our firing into them. The officer [in charge] directed me to take him to Brigade Headquarters which I did. On the way I talked with him about the war. He said he thought we should beat them in the end, that Grant was the smartest General we ever had but thought Lee of their side full as smart and called him their *Bobby Lee*. I left him at Brigade Headquarters and returned to my Regiment.

May 16-1864. Broke camp and marched about three miles to guard an ambulance train to take off the wounded of the 5th corps.[25] whose hospitals had been surrounded by the Rebs and everything movable [was] carried off together with all those who could walk.

May 17th. Left camp at twelve O'clock and moved up to the front.

May 18. About sunrize we made a charge on the Rebel works but could not drive them out so fell back with the rest of the army and we guarded the rear. Started again on the march abot 9 O'clock PM. and marched until 12. and then bivouacked for the night.

May 19th. We remained in camp all day and at night got orders to march but did not. I was on brigade guard at a place called Mary's bridge.[26] Friday May 20th. Remained in camp until about half past ten AM, and then started on a march and marched all night and until 12 O'clock the next day, [and] then built a line of works and rested.

May 21st 1864. Rested behind our works. The place is called Milford Station.[27] Sunday May 22. Very hot. Have had orders to move but did not.

May 23. Moved at 7 this morning. Had some very hard marching. Met the Rebs at 12 and were massed for a charge on the flank but did not make it.

May 24th. Left our earthworks about ten O'clock in the forenoon and crossed the North Anna river. Built more works but left them and went out on the skirmish line.

May 25. Still on the skirmish line. Built some earthworks last night and this morn strengthened them. Had heavy skirmishing all day [and had] rainy weather.

May 26th. Still on the skirmish line and raining. Left the line about ten O'clock and recrossed the North Anna river. Bivouacked behind breastworks for the night.

May 27th. This morning the Rebs got a good range on us and dropped a few shells amoungst us but we soon got under cover. Marched about 9 O'clock PM. and halted at twelve for the night.

May 28th. Marched about 6 A.M. and halted about 3 PM. a short distance from the pamunky river and supported the 5th corps who had a skirmish with the enemy. Built some works and rested for the night.

May 29-1864. Marched about noon a short distance. Built some very strong works expecting an attack but it did not come. Had orders to move about sunset but the orders were countermanded.

May thirtieth. Marched about sunrise but did not go far. Halted in the woods. Marched in line of battle across an open field and built more works.

May 31st. Moved forward again and formed another line of battle and built more works and then rested.

June 1st. Made a charge this afternoon on a line of Rebel works but could not drive them from their position. Lost a number of men [and] fell back at night.

June 2nd Marched all night last night and part of the forenoon and in the afternoon built breastworks but left them soon after. There was to of been a charge made but it was postponed on account of a heavy rain in which we were thoroughly drenched and thus we slept.

June 3-1864. Opened bright and sunney. Made a charge to day but were unsuccessful. In this charge we were formed some distance from the Rebs, and went up in Brigade front. We had not gone far before our Brigade commander was shot[28] and we being without a leader layed down. Genl. Hancock sent us word by an orderly that if those were his troops he wanted them to move forward and the Col. of the 36 Wisconsin[29] took charge and said, waiving his sword, "Forward boys!" and away we went again but had hardly got started when he fell mortally wounded. We did not go much farther as our men were falling like leaves and could not stand the fire from the Rebs. who were behind breastworks while we were in the open field, so we laid down and with bayonet and tin pan began to throw up a mound in front of us which as night drew on and with the aid of shovels developed into a formidable breastwork. We lost quite a number of our men here.[30] We are located at the extreme front being very close to the Rebel line of works and we keep completely under cover for fear of being shot. Heavy skirmishing is constantly going on and we live in fear that we may accidentaly expose some part of our body and get hit. To obtain water we dig holes 15 or 20 feet deep in a hollow near us. It is thick with clay mud but we have to use it or nothing. At night we put out our pickets and the Rebs put out theirs, and the two lines are so close together that they fire at each other and we have to take part until things get still again. Of course we can only fire at the flash of each others gun[s]. There has been several night attacks in the last week but nothing was gained on either side. When one of our men is hit by a sharpshooter here he is generally killed as only our heads show above the works when we stand upright. Our night attacks from the Rebs. generally occur after we have gone to bed and are sometimes asleep. We lay perfectly still as we have so many that we have got used to them. I hope we shall be out of this before long.

June 4th. To day we are in the same place as yesterday and our life is in constant danger. Many of the dead and wounded lay between the lines where they have lain for three or four days. At night we crawl out to some of them and drag them in laying flat on our bellies to do so. The wounded we send to the hospital and the dead we bury in this way: when we get a number of them we would dig a long treanch say 10-15-or 20 feet long 6 ft wide and two or three feet deep, [and] lay the dead in side by side, place a piece of cloth or blanket over the face and cover them up raising the ground in a long mound over them to the height of about a foot or eighteen inches.

Sometimes this was so hastily done on account of the Rebs. firing upon us that when the fall rains came they would wash away the earth and a foot or a hand would be seen protruding from the ground, when we were marching over fields that had been fought the year before; Many of the dead on this field [Cold Harbor] were buried by being covered with earth thrown out in building breastworks, the men being killed when the charge was made and the breastworks built afterwards.

June 5. To day is the blessed sabbath but war, cruel war knows no distinction of days and we are still within our breastworks which are only about thirty yards from the enemy and no part of the body can be shown without the possibility of its receiving a bullet. There was not much firing to day, only from the artillery and sharpshooters We have been compelled to dig trenches to the rear, and cover them with boughs to enable us to get water, ammunition & rations.

June 6-1864. In the same place as yesterday close up to the Rebel line. Many of our dead and wounded have lain where they fell June 3, being between the lines we are unable to get them off the field and to day a flag of truce was sent in to the Rebel lines to get permission to bring off the wounded and bury the dead. The request, after some considerable delay was granted and now each side jump up on their works without their guns and look at each other and all I can think of is mosquitoes, the men are so thick on both sides. We gradually grow bolder and finally advance toward one another, and while the stretcher bearers are carrying off the wounded, and men detailed are burying the dead, we exchange the daily papers. The flag of truce is for 24 hours and expires tomorrow at 9-A.M. It is quite a relief from being shut up in breastworks day and night.

June 7th. Everything about the same as yesterday and squads are finishing burying the dead.

June 8. Our flag of truce time has expired, but we still expose ourselves and the rebs. do the same, and no fireing is being carried on, but on the right of us and down on the left we can hear continual firing and we are of the opinion that the siege of Richmond has begun as we are distant only six miles. The weather is intensley hot.

June 9. This morning opened as usual the past three days without any firing and we exchanged papers but about 9 O'clock the rebs. told us to get under cover and the skirmishing began again. Last night after dark we quietly moved out of our breastworks in close proximity to the rebels to another line of works to the rear and on a hill and although quite near we have a much better place and have strengthened our line of works and have dug them deep enough to walk upright in and made a step in them to stand up on to fire from if the rebs should advance. We have also cut shelves in the bank to put extra cartridges in so as to give the rebs a warm reception should they try to take our works we have got a fine position, [and] skirmishing was continued all day.

June 10. To day we have again strengthened our works with logs taken from an old house. We have put the logs on top of the breastworks, and have made loop holes between them and can now fire at the rebs without being seen and we think we have also got them shell proof. Firing ceased long enough for us to exchange papers. Our night attacks have become less frequent and as a consequence we are able to get a good night's rest.

June 11. We are still in the same place and have exchanged papers after which sharpshooting was begun again and life seems to be a burden. The weather is very hot.

June 12. We were relieved by the sixth corps last night and went into camp a short distance to the rear, drew rations and remained all day. [We] moved at dark and marched most of the night. We are bound for the city of Petersburg Va.

June 13. Very pleasant and the morning finds us on the apparantly never ending march. Last night while on the march we had a scare. We were marching quietly along, too tired to talk, when all of a sudden a roaring sound was heard and in a moment more every man was jumping to the right and left. I joined suit and could only think that a body of Rebel cavalry was riding us down, but in an instant every man was getting back into line and marching on and we could hear the roaring going down the line behind us. It sounded like a tornado. We afterwards learned that an officer's horse at the head of the colum became frightened and jumped back on the line of men behind them and they in turn springing out of the way and so on until the end of the line was reached.

June 14. Broke camp about 7-A.M. and marched to Wilcox Landing on the James River where we were ferried across on steamers and landed at Windmill point[31] and marched some distance up the south bank, formed in line of battle and bivouacked for the night.

June 15-1864. Took up the line of march at twelve O'clock and had a very hard march. We marched until 11 P.M. and then halted for a rest and cooked our supper. [We] started again at 12 P.M. and again halted on a hill in the rebs works taken from them by the eighteenth corps. We got short of rations and very hungry as our supply train of wagons were unable to get up to us. We borrowed rations of the 18th corps.

June 16. We are still in the works but went out on picket a short time and had been out about four hours. We were formed in line of battle but did not advance as a line of battle of other regiments formed and advanced from our rear and we were relieved and went to the rear and supported a battery. The line of battle took the first line of works but could not get the second line and were withdrawn the next day. I think this was the first time I ever knew our corps to be engaged and we were not at the front.

June 17. We are still in the same place as yesterday with the burning sun pelting down upon us. Our Brigade was massed for a charge but we did not make it.

About this time, and for some time previous, recruits who were enlisted at the north were being sent out to the front to join the several Regiments to which they were assigned. These recruits would join us at most any time while on the march or in the breast-works in line of Battle, and some joined us at one time when we were about going into Battle. Some were wounded and some killed and we had not had time to even learn their names.

June 18-1864. Moved forward at daylight to a front line of works. Nothing of importance occured to day.

June 19. Sunday. To day is the Lords day but war knows no difference and although we have had no severe fighting there has been skirmishing all day compelling us to keep under cover.

June 20. Remained in the breastworks all day and at night were relieved by a part of the sixth corps and went to the rear and bivouacked.

June 21. Took up the line of march about noon to day. Had a short but a very hard march, advanced in skirmish line to find the strength and position of the enemy [and] halted near their rifle pits. Am in a very hard place.

June 22. After darkness set in we built a line of works to shield us from the enemy's bullets. Part of our Regt. is in line of battle in works and part are out on the skirmish line. It is a hard place. I was detailed to day to cary a dispatch to General Webb commanding our brigade, telling him the fact that we had moved to the front and connected with the line of battle on our right as we had been ordered to do and make report.[32] After delivering the dispatch and when about to return to my regiment the same way I came, Genl. Webb said to me, "Sargeant you will get hit by a sharpshooter if you return that way." I said, "No, I guess not. I came that way and was not fired at," and I started and when I got about one quarter of the way across an open field I saw a puff of smoke and a bullet struck the ground near me and before I could pop down two or three more followed in quick succession. I immediately ran under cover of some bushes and the fireing ceased. I looked at the Genl. and he was watching me. I waved my hand to him and kept under cover until I reached the regiment in the breast works. It was the only time that I could really say that I stood alone and was made a special target of by sharpshooters.

June 23. To day while lying in line of battle we were reinforced, but during a change in our lines yesterday a gap was left open and the rebs took advantage of it and captured a large number of prisoners. I will describe it as I saw it.

Our Regiment was on a rise in the ground in a piece of woods and on the right of the brigade. The left of the brigade extended across an open field into another piece of woods out of sight. The rebs had sent forward a force to feel our position and discovered the gap in the line. We heard some sharp firing in the woods and wondered what it meant, but it only lasted a few minutes. Immediately on looking over the breastworks I saw a large body of troops of our men on the move towards the rebel line. I immediately got ready to move thinking that our troops had gained a point and we should have to follow it up but we soon found out that the rebs. had captured a large number of our men and were marching them into the rebel lines, prisoners. The 15th Mass was captured almost entire.[33] [The Confederates] were finally stopped by the left of our regiment swinging around and [this] brought them to a standstill. Some of the men who escaped after being captured said that the first they know of the enemy being anywhere near them, they heard the order, "Forward 14th Alabama" and a stern command for them to throw down their guns [and] get over the breastworks and into the rebel lines and their guns were leveled at our men to cary out the order. The 7th Michigan[34] lost heavily and we also [lost] four pieces of artillery.

June 24. We moved our position to the rear and built some breast works last night. About every move we make is in the night on account of being so near the rebels. We were to be relieved by the 5th corps last night but they did not arrive until after sunrize this morning and were in plain sight of the enemy while marching up the road. Everything was quiet until they came in sight when the enemy suddenly opened a battery on [the] line. Many of the shells fell into our line and we hugged the ground to escape them but two or three of them burst right in amongst us and some of our regiment were terribly mangled in consequence. About twenty feet from where I lay a shell burst and two men were killed and several wounded. Of the two killed one had the back of his head blown completely off with his brains taken entirely out and scattered over everybody near him. The other had a large part of his left side torn off, it was a horrible sight. Those near were compelled to wipe their gun and clothes with bunches of grass of the blood and brains of their comrades. The troops that were coming up to relieve us got under cover of the wood and the firing ceased. Someone blundered. I have seen many terrible and ghastly sights on the field of battle, men with an arm or a leg torn entirely off, heads shattered in all forms, but such things are to horrible to talk about, such is war with all it terrible consequences.

The troops that were the cause of all the trouble came up and relieved us under cover of the woods and we went to the rear the same way and went into camp near a hospital. Guarding the rear, our position in this case was near the Norfolk railroad and the Jerusalem plank road.[35] From June 25th to July 16th we were encamped on the outskirts of Petersburg moving about from one place to another doing Guard, Picket and Fatigue duty at the front [and] almost constantly under fire of Rebel skirmishers and Pickets.

June 25th to July 16. A space of three weeks we remained in nearly the same place in the intrenchments around Petersburg. Gen. Hancock our corps commander having been absent wounded had now returned to us and it looks as if an active seige had begun.[36] Our regiment was now put into the first brigade.[37] We have had no heavy fighting lately but are encamped to the rear of the front line (a new place for us) and take our turn on Picket, skirmish line, building rifle pits and breastworks, now moving to the right of the line and now to the left to fill any place where needed, and to reinforce those already there. We make some hard marching amounting to 15 or 20 miles a day. We would often start just at night on a march and the break of day would find us plodding along to strike some decisive blow.

July 16-1864. Left camp about 11 O'clock last night, the night being very dark, and started on a march for somewhere, (a soldier never knows where he is going when he starts on a march and only by his own observation can he tell when he is going into a battle). We had not gone far before we found out that we had lost the road and were headed direct for the rebel lines. We halted until daylight when we again took up the line of march and finally relieved a fatigue party at work on rifle pits near a fort where we worked all day and also all the next day sunday July 17 (war knows no distinction of days) and finally got them finished and returned to camp.[38]

Monday July 18-1864. During this campaign I have been First Sargeant in charge of Companies C & E the two left flank companies of our Regiment. Now to day, July 18-1864, I have mounted and detailed my regular guard as usual about the last I shall ever detail in this regiment and I find the following entry in my diary:

"We leave for home to day, yes, Home, the dearest spot on the earth to me, how it thrills my every nerve to think of going home."

Twenty two of us who had not reenlisted and whose time expired with the regiment were called up in line about 9 O'clock this morning and turned in our guns and equipments to the Quartermaster and after receiving a few messages for the dear ones at home from the Nantucket boys, we shook hands all around and with a godspeed from all started for City Point[39] on the James river, distance about ten miles, there to take the steamer for Washington D.C. I could hardly believe that I was going home. We were in charge of Lieut Gustave Magnicksey[40] and arrived at city Point to late to take the steamer and had to stay there all night. We slept in cattle cars and it was nice compared to the way we had been sleeping (on the ground), but my thoughts were so full of home I could not sleep but little.

The next morning we took the steamer John Brooks for Washington at about ten O'clock. We were told to keep a sharp lookout as the day before the rebels had brought a battery down to the river shore and fired at the steamer but without hitting her although some of the shots came very near. I was uneasy until we arrived at Fortress Monroe at the mouth of the river. Now I had got started for home I wanted to reach there. After stopping at Fortress Monroe we left for Washington sailing all night.[41] Our bed was the after saloon deck, a palace to what we had been having. We passed Mount Vernon, the home of Washington early in the forenoon and arrived at Washington about 10 A.M. July 19th 1864. We stayed in Washington at the soldiers rest one night and left for Boston the next morning, arriving there in due season. Thence, we took the cars for Hyannis and then the steamer home. Mighty glad to get there and our friends right glad to see us. We returned to Boston [and] after a few days had a reception given us by the German Turners Association.[42] [We] were finally mustered out [and] were paid off and each one separated to look up a job for himself. I went to Brockton (then called North Bridgewater), to look for a job in the shoe business, but failing, I returned to Nantucket for a few days visit and got a chance to work in the Union store where I stayed until it broke up.

SECTION THREE

A few short anecdotes which I remember:

I have been so tired out while making forced marches at night that I would fall asleep while marching and pitch into the man in front of me which would wake me up. I have marched thirty miles at one time and we made many such marches.

In studying history of the war I find our corps, the 2nd Army Corps, was put to the front on almost every occassion.[1] Our Genl. [Hancock] was considered one of the smartest in the army. He was a fine looking man of about 6 foot tall.

While we were in camp at Falmouth Va. during the winter of 1862-3, we did picket duty on the banks of the Rappahanock river. One day an ox who had been driven out to be slaughtered stampeded after being shot at, and not hit, and made a break from the river into which he plunged, and was making his way across to the rebel side (the river being low and easily forded), when the rebs espied him and began to shout at the the prospect of having some fresh meat. But when about two thirds of the way over [the ox] stopped at hearing such a noise. We immediately got under cover and he returned to the shore on our side and was shot there, the rebs looking on from their side in silence. Had they kept under cover he would undoubtedly have gone clear across. While in this camp our men would shout across to the johnnies to bring over some tobacco and swap for coffee and they would meet half way in the river and exchange coffee for tobacco and also exchange papers. We were within rifle range of each other all winter and spring, but no firing was done across the river.

On the march from Boliver Heights to Falmouth Va in Nov. 1862 we had some cool nights and would frequently wake up in the morning with our hair and blankets covered with frost. Snow fell in one or two instances and Ice formed quite thick, and we, sleeping on the ground with no tents of any kind to shield us. How we ever survived these things I cannot tell.

When we crossed the Rappahanock river in boats at the assault on Fredericksburg, it was necessary to push the boats a little way from the shore to prevent their grounding when we got into them. The shore was fringed with ice and we with shoes on, of course, we were wet above our ancles and with no chance to dry them and this in the month of December, 1862.

In reading different histories of the war I frequently see places mentioned where it says that the faces of the dead were covered by some kind friend, which was true but many of them were covered as I have covered them while standing in line of battle engaging the enemy.

A comrade will be shot down next to you or very near while you keep on firing. In a few moments, you will look at the dead comrade and find him with his eyes wide open and glassy, staring into vacancy. A strange feeling comes over you and you will stoop down and cover the face with the cape of his overcoat, his blouse, or any piece of cloth that comes handy, shutting out the sight.

I had often heard our men who had been wounded speak of the horrors of a field hospital on the night after a battle and it is certainly true as my experience tells me. The first night I spent in the Lacy House hospital opposite Fredericksburg was an awful night.

Men were brought in at all hours of the night with all kinds of wounds and groaning terribly. Others were brought in from the battlefield insensible but also groaning with pain. Those that died during the night were carried out and laid on the ground to make room for others.

The soldier who layed next to me when I was wounded, was wounded in the hip and was a confederate of the 13th Miss. Regt. The man next to him was a Union soldier with a ball in his brain, insensible, the brain oozing out of the hole made by the bullet. A man was brought in on a stretcher with a terrible shell wound on the under side of the upper part of his right leg. Pieces of flesh hung down two inches long. He bled to death in a short time. In the room next to me was a rebel of the 8th Florida Regt. with both feet taken off at the ancles.[2] There were also men wounded right through the lungs. In another room the surgeons were amputating and the arms and legs that were cut off formed quite a pile in front of the hospital. they were afterwards buried.

Our principle food while on a campaign was salt pork, hard bread, coffee and dark brown sugar and we would have this for weeks at a time, and once in a while, we would get a ration of fresh beef, and when a battle lasted all day we would eat our food of salt pork and hardbread, and drink water during a lull in the battle. No attention was paid to meals while on a march because we eat while marching and get our meals when we could.

While in camp at Brandy Station on the Orange and Alexandria Railroad[3] near Petersburg Va. our division was called on to witness the hanging of a soldier named Thomas R. Dawson for the crime of committing rape on a old lady who died from the affect of the crime. It was in 1864.[4] We formed in a double hollow square[5] with the scaffold in the centre. The soldier was driven inside in a team sitting on his coffin with his arms pinioned at his elbows. He seemed not to have the slightest fear and ascended the steps of the scaffold with a firm tread. His excuse was that he was drunk and did not know what he was doing.

While on the scaffold the charges and sentence were read to him after which he stepped forward on the trap and looked down to see if he was square on the trap. Before the cap was drawn down he was asked if he had anything to say and he said simply this: "You may break my neck but you cannot break my manly spirit." The cap was drawn down when he took out his handkerchief and kept turning it around in his hands, showing some nervousness. The trap was sprung and he was launched into eternity making only one movement which was a contraction of the whole body. After that, all was still and the body swung around in the wind. He hung thirty minutes and was then cut down, placed in the coffin and buried just to the right of the scaffold, his grave having been previously dug and in plain sight of him from the scaffold. The place where he was executed was on the plantation of John Minor Botts.[6] While in camp at Brandy station on the Orange and Alexander R.R., we used to go out on picket and stay 3 days at a time, about three miles from camp. In the woods we built coverings of pine boughs to break off the wind and rain and would make immense fires of oak logs to keep warm. We would frequently have a rain that would last the whole three days and were wet through nearly the whole time. I cannot see how we ever lived through it.

At the Battle of Spottsylvania fought May 12th 1864, we were stationed in front of the salient or as it is sometimes called the "bloody angle," endeavoring to drive the rebels out. But they were strongly posted and we were on the outside and could not dislodge them. I thought possible I might start the boys on a charge to dislodge them as we were losing men fast (being in the open field and they behind [the Confederate] works) and gaining nothing, I seized my cap and running out in front of our line cried out, "Lets charge up there and drive them out!" but I could not start them and the firing continued as before this was after Kelley and the others were taken prisoners.

Taken into consideration the men engaged on both sides the number of bullets fired together with the grape, shot, cannister, solid shot and shells, and it is a wonder to me how any of us ever got out alive.

One thing is that the impenetrable smoke that hangs over a battle-field almost shuts out the position of the enemy.

In going into the battle of the Wilderness it was necessary to double quick to reach a position before the rebels did. I began to fall behind on account of my load and to keep up had to throw away my knapsack for which I was ever afterwards sorry as it contained a rubber pillow I bought when I came home with Lieut. Alley's body and a few other things which it was impossible for me to replace. My pillow after that consisted of the flat side of my tin plate inside my haversack, rather hard but the best I had. I got another knapsack on the field after the fight was over but not as good. I brought it home with me and have it now together with my canteen, rubber blanket, cup and plate.

Our commanding officer, Henry L. Abbott, would say to us, "When in battle, to fire low boys," reasoning that a wounded man was equal to three dead ones because if a man was wounded there was a good chance of two of his comrades helping him off the field which took three from the line.

Sometimes fresh meat would be issued to us just before we started on the march. Then, as we could not cary it and had no chance to cook it, we would eat it raw.

After every battle in which we were engaged we would come out of it with our mouth and faces and hands blackened with powder. We had to bite off the cartridges in those days to enable us to pour the powder into our guns.

After almost every battle we would have a rain storm and often while we were fighting it would be raining and where the wounded and killed lay a little stream of crimson water would flow, telling too truely the result which would follow.

Our division was one called to witness the shooting of a deserter but we were hardly near enough to witness the whole of it.

At one time two men from our company were detailed to act as a reserve at the shooting of a deserter in case he was not killed at the first discharge and it happened he was not and these two men were compelled to do the disagreeable duty of going close up to him and firing at his head to end his misery. One of them was a Nantucket man since dead so I will not mention his name although at one time he was town clerk of this Town.[7]

Deserters are shot in this way after trial by Court martial and sentenced. They are marched to the place of execution, their hands tied behind them and eyes blindfolded, and then seated on their coffin, are shot. Twelve muskets are loaded by a sargeant one of which has a blank charge, the soldiers not knowing which one of them has the blank cartridge, so of course no one knows who shot him.

Soldiers could hardly keep any run of what day of the week it was while on a campaign and all days seemed alike when on the march. we often fought over battles on sunday the same as any other day. We marched and fought Sundays and nights in sunshine and rain. When it rained we got wet and waited for the sun to come out and dry us.

While on the march to Spottsylvania, we made a charge late one afternoon and were unsuccessful. We then marched all night without any sleep and made another charge at daylight the next morning, and fought all day getting no sleep until midnight. What food we ate, we ate right from our haversacks.

We slept always with our clothes on to help keep warm and be ready for any emergency.

When we have gatherings in celebrating the reinstated and perpetual union they include the men who bore the heat and struggle of the battle, who did the fighting and endured the hardship, who carried the musket the canteen and the knapsack, the private [illegible] soldier

The Officers are all right, they did their duty as became Patriots and brave men. But they had many compensations which were beyond the reach of the rank and file. Fame beckoned to them and glory waited on their deeds. They had comforts, even luxuries to sustain them in health, and tenderist care in sickness and in suffering. The Private soldier rejoiced in none of these.

Love of country and of flag was his incentive.

Footsore and famished in unnoticed patience.

He stood a lonely sentinal through nights of terror and of pain. He fought in the forefront of the battle with peril for his company and death or mutilation awaiting the end. His nameless headstones dot a hundred southern hills, and peaceful harvests laugh above his scattered bones. To his memory, if dead, and in his honor if surviving, this splendid nation which his valor saved, should offer the tribute of its greatest reverence.

At once the victim and the hero of the tragedy of thirty years ago, he is the worthiest object of our thoughts.

Time will thin the Veteran ranks, as battle thinned the armies of thirty years ago, and each succeeding year will illustrate the mournful record of their mortality. But never so long as Americans love liberty, and honor the precepts of their fathers will America forget her debt to the private soldier who fought with Grant and Sheridan and Sherman with Hancock and Thomas and Meade and to whose courage and fidelity under every trial the country owes its present happiness and peace.

In the year 1891 a majority of the survivors of the war of this town formed a Grand Army Post. I was made Officer of the Day and afterwards elected Post Commander in which office I served three years in succession. The Post was named Thomas M. Gardner Post 207 G.A.R. It is in being to day and I am its Post Comr. for the second time. We have only 11 members. The rest are dead. Mar 1919.

[This entry appears in Murphey's handwriting on an unnumbered page]:

The following is a list of Battles in which I was engaged this does not include skirmishes which would more than double the list.

South Mountain Maryland under fire but not engaged.

Antietam Sept 17-1862 lost 148 men

Fredericksburg Dec. 11 1862 where I was wounded.

Chancellorsville May 2-1863. we fought in this Battle at Fredericksburg city

Rapidan reconoisance under fire but not engaged.

Wilderness, May 6-7-8-1864

Todds Tavern May 9-1864

Laurel Hill May 10-1864 where Lieut. Sturges just transferred from the 34th N.Y. was killed on shady grove road

Po River.

Spottsylvania May 12-1864 where I was sixteen continuous hours under fire

Spottsylvania May 18-1864 near the Landron house hardly any troops but the 1st & 2nd div. of our corps engaged, this was where I carried dispatches to the rear and was made a special target of by rebels at North Anna river May 24-1864

Totopotomony June 1-1864

Cold Harbor June 2 to 12-1864 under fire in breast works for ten days. 3000 men fell in our corps on June 2nd in 22 minutes in a charge attack made every night after dark

Petersburg June 16

Jerusalem plank road 21st June with South Mountain & Todds Tavern makes 13 hard fought battles not including 10 consecutive days under fire at cold harbor where we had a skirmish nearly every night on account of the pickets being so near to each other.

NOTES TO MEMOIRS

Section One [Pp. 71–94]

1. Hardee's *Rifle and Light Infantry Tactics*, a military instruction manual widely used during the war, characterizes the rank of orderly, or first sergeant, as the "most important one" of all noncommissioned officers, and includes among its responsibilities the forming of the company for all drills and parades, calling the roll, making sick reports, supervising details of all company duties, drawing rations for the company, and issuing clothing as needed. "When in action," Hardee states, "the noncommissioned officers will assist the officers in maintaining discipline, in keeping the men in the ranks, and will enforce obedience, if necessary."

2. Murphey enlisted for either the duration of the war or the unexpired term of his regiment, whichever was earlier. In August 1864, the 20th Massachusetts' original three-year term expired and Murphey returned to Boston for discharge.

3. Arthur H. Gardner, 1855–1924. State legislator from Nantucket and editor of the Nantucket *Journal*.

4. Battle of Antietam, September 17–18, 1862. Near Sharpsburg, Maryland, Union forces halted Confederate General Robert E. Lee's first invasion of the North, forcing his return to Virginia.

5. The Union Store was a Nantucket grocery at the corner of Main and Centre streets.

6. Charles H. Bailey, 1810–83. Nantucket merchant.

7. Frank J. Crosby, 1835–1903. A Nantucket selectman who was appointed by Massachusetts Governor John A. Andrew as the island's recruiting officer. Pantheon Hall was on the second floor in the building next to the Union Store.

8. Situated in North Cambridge, Massachusetts, Camp Cameron was described by William Schouler, Governor Andrew's adjutant general, as a "general rendezvous for recruits intended for regiments already in the field."

9. The Soldiers' Retreat was a rest stop maintained in Washington, D.C., for soldiers traveling to and from the capital. One contemporary source described it as an "eating house."

10. General John Pope, 1822–92. In June 1862, Lincoln named Pope, an 1842 graduate of West Point, as commander of the short-lived Federal Army of Virginia. He was defeated by Confederate General Thomas J. "Stonewall" Jackson at the battle of Second Manassas and was relieved of his command shortly thereafter.

11. Barbara Fritchie was a 95-year-old resident of Frederick, Maryland, and the heroine of the John Greenleaf Whittier poem bearing her name. According to lore, she waved the national flag as Stonewall Jackson and his troops passed through Frederick on September 6, 1962, en route to Antietam. One version has it that the normally fierce Jackson was so impressed by Fritchie's bravery that he removed his cap as a gesture of respect. The story is doubted by most historians.

12. Battle of South Mountain, September 14, 1862. Preliminary to Antietam, the battle

of South Mountain was an effort by the Federal IX Corps to trap part of Lee's divided army at Turner's Gap, a key pass through the Blue Ridge Mountains. Union losses at South Mountain totaled 1,813, consisting of 325 killed, 1,403 wounded, and 85 missing. Estimates of Confederate losses total 2,685 men consisting of 325 killed, 1,560 wounded, and 800 missing. The 20th Massachusetts was negligibly engaged.

13. Jesse Lee Reno, 1823–62. An 1846 graduate of West Point, Major General Reno led the Union IX Corps at South Mountain, where he was killed in action.

14. Murphey and his fellow recruits were not issued rifles. Sergeant John Summerhayes of Company I, in a letter published by the Nantucket *Weekly Mirror* on October 11, 1862, provided this account of how his men obtained them: "As we marched forward to [Antietam], Lieut. Alley ordered us to pick up all the muskets we could find on the road, and take them away from all the stragglers. We did so, and by the time we formed our line of battle all were equipped. Some had one kind of musket and some another; some would have bayonets and some not; some would have their rounds of cartridges in their pockets, and some had them in a cartridge box with the caps in their pockets."

15. Robert Edward Lee, 1807–70. An 1829 graduate of West Point, Lee commanded the Confederate Army of Northern Virginia from June 1862 until the surrender at Appomattox.

16. Estimates of the 20th Massachusetts' casualties at Antietam range from 124 to 148. Company I's share was one dead and one wounded. Total Federal casualties for Antietam were 12,410: 2,108 killed, 9,549 wounded, and 753 missing. Confederate losses totaled 13,724 of which 2,700 were killed, 9,024 were wounded and approximately 2,000 missing.

17. John Brown, 1800–59, was the revolutionary abolitionist and leader of the abortive attempt to seize the Federal arsenal at Harpers Ferry, on October 16, 1859.

18. Waves of typhoid fever and dysentery swept through the 20th Massachusetts following this march. Between October 1862 and April 1863, disease would kill three members of Company I and result in the discharges of twenty-nine more.

19. Town near Harpers Ferry. Described by the 20th Massachusetts' official regimental historian as "pleasantly located on the brow of the hill from which there was a beautiful view, and where the air was pure and bracing."

20. Lincoln, deeply disturbed by McClellan's failure to pursue Lee after Antietam, decided to visit the Army of the Potomac's commanding general in the field. While there, he reviewed the troops, which included the 20th Massachusetts.

21. Libby Prison was a Confederate prisoner-of-war facility located in a converted warehouse in Richmond, Virginia. Intended for Union officers, it held 1300 men, and as in so many other such prisons North and South, conditions were primitive.

22. Andersonville was the most infamous of all the Civil War prisoner-of-war camps in a conflict that saw abominable treatment of prisoners on both sides of the Mason-Dixon Line. Located near Anderson, Georgia, the camp was an open-air facility originally designed to hold a population of 10,000 Union prisoners, which quickly swelled to 33,000 of which one-third perished, mostly from disease.

23. Fredericksburg, Virginia, is a town on the Rappahannock River midway between Washington, D.C., and Richmond. It was the site of Confederate General Robert E. Lee's defeat of Union forces commanded by General Ambrose E. Burnside, December 11–13, 1862.

24. On October 16, 1862, the 20th Massachusetts participated in an expedition at Charles Town, Virginia. Resistance was token, and the regiment suffered no casualties. Charles Town is the scene of the trial and execution of John Brown.

25. George B. McClellan, 1826–85. An 1846 graduate of West Point, McClellan was appointed by Lincoln as commander of the Army of the Potomac following the Federal disaster at the First Manassas. Although a brilliant administrator, McClellan lacked the aggressiveness necessary for combat command. He was relieved by Lincoln shortly after Antietam.

26. Ambrose E. Burnside, 1824–81. An 1847 graduate of West Point, Burnside was appointed by Lincoln to succeed McClellan as commander of the Army of the Potomac. The assault on Fredericksburg was conceived by Burnside, and following its failure he was replaced by Major General Joseph Hooker.

27. The 50th New York Engineers was one of three engineer regiments assigned to build the pontoon bridges on which Burnside's army was to cross the Rappahannock. The 50th New York was assigned to build the bridge leading directly into the town. Confederate sharpshooters delayed construction for almost twelve hours, until they were forced to withdraw by Union forces crossing the river in boats.

28. William Buel Franklin, 1823–1903. An 1843 graduate of West Point, Franklin commanded the Left Grand Division of the Union army at Fredericksburg, one of three grand divisions. The 20th Massachusetts belonged to the Right Grand Division.

29. Ira Spaulding, commander of the 50th New York Engineers, described the conditions facing his bridge builders: "At about 6:00 AM . . . the enemy opened a galling fire upon us at the upper bridges, from the houses near the shore and from behind walls and fences, killing 1 captain and two men and wounding several others. One bridge had approached so near the south shore that the men at work upon it were within 80 yards of the enemy, who were under cover, while the infantry supporting us on the flanks were at long range, and could do little damage to the enemy. My men were working without arms; had no means of returning the enemy's fire, and were driven from the work. (*The War of the Rebellion: A Compilation of the Official Records of the Union and Confederate Armies* (hereinafter *OR*), Series I, Vol. XXI (Washington, Government Printing Office, 1888), pp. 177–79.) Spaulding said his men were driven back three times by enemy fire. The Confederates claimed they drove them back nine times.

30. Colonel Norman J. Hall commanded the brigade to which the 20th Massachusetts belonged and which included Hall's own 7th Michigan, the 19th Massachusetts, the 42nd New York, and the 59th New York. It was never intended that the 20th Massachusetts should cross in boats. Colonel Hall explained: "An order for the Twentieth Massachusetts Volunteers to move across the bridge the moment it was down was incorrectly transmitted, so as to cause Acting Major Macy, its commanding officer, to throw it across in boats." [*OR,* I, XXI, 282–85.] Macy was responsible for recruiting Nantucketers into

Company I and eventually rose to command the regiment. Breveted a Major General of Volunteers, he was the highest ranking officer Nantucket produced during the war. See Roster, p. 166.

31. George Henry Boker, 1823–1890. A poet, dramatist, and diplomat, Boker was United States Minister to Turkey, 1871–75, and Minister to Russia, 1875–79. The poem was inspired by one of Murphey's better-known comrades in the 20th Massachusetts, Captain Oliver Wendell Holmes, Jr. A future associate justice on the United States Supreme Court, Holmes was hospitalized with dysentery during the battle of Fredericksburg. Later, while recuperating at the home of a friend in Philadelphia, he met Boker. The poem is written from the point of view of a bedridden officer who is forced to lie helplessly in hospital while his comrades carry the waterborne assault.

32. Thomas J. Russell, 1842–1923, was a fellow Nantucketer and Company I comrade of Murphey's in the 20th Massachusetts. See Roster, p. 183.

33. Leander F. Alley, 1833–62, also a Nantucketer, rose from the ranks in the 20th Massachusetts to become a second lieutenant. See Roster, p. 136.

34. See Murphey's drawing, page 88.

35. Henry Livermore Abbott, 1842–64. Scion of a wealthy Lowell, Massachusetts, family, Abbott enlisted in the 20th Massachusetts in 1861 as a first lieutenant of Company I and eventually rose to a brief command of the regiment in the battle of the Wilderness. Like many of the patrician officers with the 20th Massachusetts, his politics were Federalist-Democrat. With pride, Abbott once described the 20th Massachusetts as the "Copperhead Regiment," a reference to those Northerners who opposed Lincoln's war policy and were strongly anti-abolitionist. He was highly regarded on Nantucket, where families of the injured and dead could always expect a letter from him. The regard was mutual. On his death, Abbott bequeathed money to Nantucket families left destitute due to the loss of a loved one in the war.

36. See Murphey's drawing, page 88.

37. The Lacy House was a mansion on the north side of the Rappahannock. During the battle of Fredericksburg, the house was used as headquarters by Major General Edwin V. Sumner, commander of the Right Grand Division, and also as a hospital.

38. As quoted in *OR* , I, XXI, 283–84.

39. The 20th Massachusetts' casualties at Fredericksburg totaled 163 killed and wounded. The regiment entered the fray with 335 effectives, resulting in a casualty rate of nearly fifty percent.

40. Before the battle of Fredericksburg, Company I totaled sixty effectives. Approximately thirty became casualties between December 11 and 13, 1862. All but two occurred during the river crossing and in the street fighting. Eighteen were Nantucketers.

41. The 13th Mississippi was one of four Mississippi regiments constituting Barksdale's Brigade, named after its commander, Brigadier General and former United States congressman William Barksdale, 1821–63. This brigade held the south bank of the Rappahannock on December 11, frustrating Federal attempts to complete the Upper Bridge.

What Murphey may not have known was that Confederate Lieutenant Lane Brandon of the 21st Mississippi, also of Barksdale's Brigade, was a Harvard classmate and friend of Henry L. Abbott. When Brandon discovered that the Federal advance was led by Abbott, he stiffened his resistance and, against orders, led a counterattack that briefly repulsed Company I. For this, Lieutenant Brandon was placed under arrest.

42. Ball's Bluff is on the Potomac River near Leesburg, Virginia. It was the site of the first battle of the 20th Massachusetts, a Federal disaster. The regiment's casualties were 13 killed in action, 15 mortally wounded, 25 wounded, and 228 missing. Most of the missing were taken prisoner by the Confederates.

43. Fair Oaks is a town near Richmond, Virginia, near a battle fought on May 31, 1862, during McClellan's Peninsula Campaign. The 20th Massachusetts had casualties of five killed and mortally wounded.

44. The man is not identified.

45. Acquia Creek Landing is on the south bank of the upper Potomac River, approximately fifteen miles northeast of Fredericksburg.

46. Aggregate Union losses at Fredericksburg were 12,653: 1,284 killed, 9,600 wounded, including mortally wounded, and 1,769 captured or missing. Confederate casualties are estimated at 5,315: 596 killed, 4,068 wounded, and 651 captured or missing.

47. Sergeant John Summerhayes provided this account of the retrieval of Alley's body: "I shall never forget when [Captain Abbott] asked for Volunteers to go after [Alley's body]. When he, Alley, was struck down I was out on the right, with Six sharpshooters in front of a Battery and Rifle Pit, picking off Gunners and keeping their [the enemy's] skirmishers from firing on our right wing, the heaviest part of the battle was over, and the night shadows were falling, shells exploding lit up the hill [Marye's Heights] like flashes of lightening [sic]—Sergt. Holmes came creeping up to my post—"Summerhayes! Alley's killed, I am to relieve you as the Capt. wishes your Services." This was his greeting, you can imagine my feelings—I have seen a good many men die—Some Comrades, and it has not caused a nerve to tremble—but those words made a demon of me; in an instant I was on my feet. I pity the Greyback whether well, sick or wounded who should have fallen into my hands then. . . ." ("Letters of a Soldier in the Civil War," *Massachusetts Magazine,* reprint, n.d. Original in archives of the Nantucket Historical Association, Nantucket, Massachusetts.) Summerhayes also remarks on Murphey's journey home with Alley's body: "Was glad to hear that Murphy was used so well—he is a good boy and I think did his duty—receiving his wound in the first part of the street fight he had little chance to see much of the details, yet he can enlighten you in a measure as to the wounded and dead of Nantucket."

See Roster, p. 136, for Leander F. Alley.

48. The Sanitary Commission and the Christian Commission were private relief organizations dedicated to the welfare of Union soldiers.

49. Eight Nantucketers were killed at Fredericksburg: Leander F. Alley, Charles F. Ellis, Charles A. Morris, George E. Snow, Clinton Swain, Jacob G. Swain, William H. Wilcomb, and William H. Winslow.

50. The father and son are not identified.

51. Phebe Ann Hanaford, 1829–1921. Hanaford, born on Nantucket, was a poet, a Universalist minister, and the first female pastor in New England.

Section Two [pp. 95–114]

1. Commander of Camp Cameron.

2. William R. Riddle joined Company I as a first sergeant in July 1861. He was promoted to second lieutenant in October 1861 and was discharged for disability in September 1863 with the rank of first lieutenant. He lost his arm at Ball's Bluff.

3. The Chancellorsville campaign began in early May 1863. Hooker, now commanding the Army of the Potomac, attempted to deceive Lee by ordering the II Corps to make a feint toward the town of Fredericksburg, while the rest of the army effected a wide circling movement ultimately to cross the Rappahannock nearly twenty miles up the river at Kelly's Ford. This time, Lee's formidable works at Marye's Heights were drained of their defenders as he shifted forces to meet Hooker's principal thrust. Union forces captured the Heights, but were ordered to withdraw across the river after Hooker's defeat. The casualties of the 20th Massachusetts were two killed and thirteen wounded.

4. The Washington Artillery was a Confederate regiment consisting of wealthy and prominent men from New Orleans.

5. General Robert E. Lee's second invasion of the North took the Army of Northern Virginia through Maryland and into Pennsylvania, culminating in the battle of Gettysburg.

6. Baptist Branch Hospital in Washington D.C.

7. The Mine Run campaign, November 26 to December 1, 1863, was an attempt by Union commander George G. Meade to cross the Rapidan River and outmaneuver Robert E. Lee by the flank and rear. But Confederate cavalry General J.E.B. Stuart heard of the plan and strongly entrenched his positions along Mine Run. Meade wished to avoid another Fredericksburg, and the attack on Stuart's positions was canceled.

8. On December 7, 1863, the 20th Massachusetts moved from Stevensburg, Virginia, to nearby Cole's Hill. It remained there until the Wilderness Campaign the following May.

9. The Wilderness Campaign, May 5–7, 1864, began the spring offensive by the Union army directed by newly appointed Lieutenant General Ulysses S. Grant. Grant crossed the Rapidan River with 101,895 infantry, and immediately encountered Lee's army in an impenetrable brush forest. Murphey's date of May 2 is an error; the 20th Massachusetts marched on May 3.

10. Ulysses Simpson Grant, 1822–85. An 1843 graduate of West Point, Grant first distinguished himself in the western theater of the war directing the capture of Forts Henry and Donaldson, the battles of Shiloh and Vicksburg, and the relief of Chattanooga. On March 9, 1864, Lincoln appointed Grant as Lieutenant General of All the Armies, the first to hold that office since George Washington. Grant served two terms as President, from 1868 to 1876.

11. Winfield Scott Hancock, 1824–86. An 1840 graduate of West Point, Hancock commanded the Union II Corps from Gettysburg until he was wounded at the battle of Spotsylvania. Murphey's high opinion of Hancock was widely shared throughout the army.

12. One of several fords crossing the Rapidan River.

13. The 20th Massachusetts lost 43 killed and 173 wounded at the Wilderness and Spotsylvania. Included among the dead was Acting Colonel Henry Livermore Abbott.

14. William Fuchs enlisted in the 20th Massachusetts as a private in July 1861. A member of Company C, Fuchs was promoted to sergeant by the time of the Wilderness Campaign, where he was wounded.

15. George Gordon Meade, 1815–72. An 1835 graduate of West Point, Meade was commander of the Army of the Potomac from shortly before Gettysburg through the end of the war. Following Grant's appointment as lieutenant general, Meade reported directly to Grant.

16. Todd's Tavern was located about one mile south of the southern edge of the Wilderness, at the intersection of the Brock and Orange Court House roads. From May 5 to 9, it was the site of continuous fighting.

17. Spotsylvania Court House is a Virginia townsite south of the Wilderness and the scene of fierce fighting, May 8 to 21, 1864. Spotsylvania was the next major battle following the Wilderness in Grant's and Lee's struggle for control of Virginia. The 20th Massachusetts lost twenty men killed.

18. Edward "Allegheny" Johnson, 1816–73. An 1838 graduate of West Point, Johnson was a Confederate general who held various military commands during the war.

19. George H. "Maryland" Steuart, 1828–1903. An 1848 graduate of West Point, Steuart was a Confederate general commanding at various times both infantry and cavalry units.

20. The captain of the New York regiment is unidentified.

21. Murphey is referring to the Bloody Angle, a salient in Lee's fortifications at Spotsylvania and the focus of Grant's attack. The twenty-hour battle fought there on May 11–12, 1864, was at times at such close quarters that rifles could be used only as clubs. In some places, the dead were piled seven deep.

22. William P. Kelley, 1843–65. A Nantucket comrade of Murphey's and sergeant in Company I of the 20th Massachusetts. See Roster, p. 164.

23. The road is unidentified.

24. Murphey is probably mistaken about the identity of his prisoner's unit. The 39th Georgia is not listed in the Army of Northern Virginia's order of battle for the period indicated.

25. The V Corps was one of twenty-five Union army corps existing at one time or another during the war. A corps is generally defined as an army unit of organization consisting of two or more divisions.

26. Mary's Bridge crosses the Ny River about three miles north of Spotsylvania Court House.

27. Milford Station is a Virginia town on the Mattaponi River, through which the 20th Massachusetts marched en route to Cold Harbor.

28. Brigadier General Alexander S. Webb, 1835–1911. An 1855 graduate and mathematics professor at West Point, Webb participated in every major battle of the Army of the Potomac until his wounding at Spotsylvania, where a statue of him was erected after the war. Highly regarded by his men, he received the Medal of Honor for his defense of another Bloody Angle, the point on the Union lines where Pickett's Charge crested at Gettysburg.

29. Colonel Frank A. Haskell of the 36th Wisconsin was killed a short time after assuming command. The 36th Wisconsin was a late-war regiment formed in March 1864 and sent to Spotsylvania Court House on May 10, 1864. It was brigaded with the 20th Massachusetts through Lee's surrender at Appomattox.

30. Federal casualties from the assault at Cold Harbor totaled 12,737: 1,844 killed, 9,077 wounded and mortally wounded, and 1,816 captured or missing. The 20th Massachusetts' casualties were twelve killed or mortally wounded.

31. Wilcox Landing and Windmill Point are opposite each other on the north and south banks of the James River.

32. Although Murphey identifies the general as Webb, the brigade commander on June 22 could only have been either Brigadier General B. R. Pierce or Major W. F. Smith of the First Delaware Infantry. General Webb was absent because of his wound at Spotsylvania. As June 22 was the day Pierce was replaced by Smith, it is unclear which man Murphey would have reported to.

33. Forty-seven men of the 15th Massachusetts were taken prisoner by the Confederates near Petersburg.

34. The 7th Michigan had been brigaded with the 20th Massachusetts for several years.

35. The Norfolk and Petersburg Railroad ran southeast of Petersburg and connected that city with Suffolk and Norfolk, Virginia. The Jerusalem Plank Road was a major highway connecting Petersburg with points south.

36. Major General W. S. Hancock returned to briefly command II Corps on June 27 and remained until November 26, 1864.

37. The 20th Massachusetts had been transferred to First Brigade from Second Brigade in March 1864, although it remained in the Second Division of Second Corps.

38. Although the fort is unidentified, this period saw the 20th Massachusetts join in the army-wide effort to strengthen the entrenchments at Petersburg.

39. City Point, Virginia, was a town on the James River near Petersburg. It became a supply port and rail depot for Grant's army during the siege of Petersburg and Richmond, 1864–65.

40. Gustave Magnitzky, an immigrant from Polish Prussia, joined the 20th Massachusetts in July 1861 as a sergeant in Company G. Wounded at Gettysburg, he was later promoted to captain for gallantry in action. He was a favorite of Captain Oliver Wendell

Holmes, Jr., and after the war he was office manager for the Boston law firm of Shattuck, Holmes and Monroe for over 40 years.

41. Fort Monroe was at the tip of Yorktown Peninsula, Virginia, and was held by Union forces throughout the war.

42. The German Turners Association was a private organization of gymnasts.

Section Three [pp. 114–21]

1. It is difficult to argue with Murphey's statement. Fox says in *Regimental Losses:*

"The Second Corps was prominent by reason of its longer and continuous service, larger organization, hardest fighting, and greatest number of casualties. Within its ranks was the regiment which sustained the largest percentage of loss in any one action; also, the regiment which sustained the greatest numerical loss during its term of service; while, of the one hundred regiments in the Union army which lost the most men in battle, thirty five of them belonged to the Second Corps." Fox concludes: "The history of the Second Corps was identical with that of the Army of the Potomac. It needs no word of praise; its record was unsurpassed."

2. The 8th Florida had been assigned to Barksdale's Brigade to defend the town of Fredericksburg.

3. Brandy Station is situated on the Orange & Alexandria Railroad, midway between Culpepper Court House and the North Fork of the Rappahannock River.

4. On April 24, 1864, Thomas R. Dawson of Company I was hanged for his part in the rape of an elderly woman. Dawson claimed that he and two other men were intoxicated when the crime was committed. The case was appealed to President Lincoln, who allowed the execution to proceed. The priest who administered last rites to the condemned remembered a botched hanging, which accounts for the jerking Murphey observed when the trap was sprung: ". . . the provost marshal misjudged the length of the rope being used. When the trapdoor sprung, [Dawson] fell to a standing position on the ground. A frantic executioner seized the end of the rope and jerked the prisoner upward until death slowly came." It is interesting to note that Dawson fought for Britain in the Crimean War and was said to have been awarded the Victoria Cross and the Cross of Honor.

5. A double-hollow square is an infantry formation in which the men form two rectangles, one within the other with the distance between both lines not exceeding the regulation length of thirteen inches. The gallows is in the center, and the double-hollow formation allowed each man to witness the execution

6. John Minor Botts, 1802–69, was a Virginia unionist and politician, having served three terms in the antebellum Congress.

7. Murphey wrote the name "Samuel Christian" above the words "town clerk." Samuel Christian, 1833–75, enlisted with Murphey in the 20th Massachusetts in August 1862. He returned to Nantucket and did serve as town clerk. See Roster, p. 151.

IV Roster of

Nantucket Men

in Company I

20th Massachusetts

Volunteer Infantry

Introduction to the Roster

IT SEEMS IMPOSSIBLE TO SPEAK OF THE IMPACT OF WAR on a community without a resort to cases. The horrors of the Civil War, with its appalling casualties, primitive medicine, disease, hardships, and death can perhaps be understood only by recounting the experiences of the men who, as Lincoln said, "shall have borne the battle."

The Nantucketers of Company I of the 20th Massachusetts were certainly among those who bore the battle. They were obscure, mostly poor men, and the authors feared that the mission of bringing them to life would founder upon, as the poet Thomas Gray observed, "the short and simple annals of the poor." In fact, many sources were available in compiling this roster. The starting point was the military and pension records stored at the National Archive and Records Administration in Washington, D. C. America had never fought a war as big as the Civil War, and the government's need to process some 2,800,000 enlistments and millions of pension claims after the war ensured that ordinary soldiers (and many of their families) were to become the first generation of well-documented Americans.

Still, by contemporary standards, Civil War records are often inconsistent, incomplete, and erroneous. Information about promotions, injuries, sickness, and physical characteristics is not available for all soldiers and is sometimes inaccurate where it appears. Official entries of "desertion" should be viewed with suspicion. Many soldiers excusedly absent due to sickness, wounds, or detached duty were frequently marked as "deserted" by ignorant record keepers; the authors have attempted to identify actual desertions. As a rule, officers have thicker files than enlisted personnel, and details of their promotions, furloughs, and other activities seem to have merited more attention from the record keepers.

Pension records are by far the most interesting of the official documents. To establish a claim, soldiers had to submit extensive evidence regarding wartime service, injuries, illnesses, and current medical condition. The documentation was usually verified by the Bureau of Pensions, resulting in mountains of useful information not included in military records. Surviving relatives of deceased soldiers frequently had to prove their relationship, which was sometimes done through letters that had been written by the soldier to the claimant and which, fortunately for historians, the Bureau of Pensions often retained as part of the permanent file. Birth, death, and marriage records are also present in many pension files.

Nantucket boasted two newspapers during the Civil War, the Nantucket *Weekly Mirror* and the Nantucket *Inquirer*. Both provide essential information about individuals. Each regularly printed correspondence from Nantucket soldiers that consciously strove to communicate news about other islanders at "the seat of the war." Whenever possible, the papers printed letters of condolence from company commanders to the families of deceased soldiers containing valuable details about how they died or comported themselves as soldiers. Finally, both newspapers carried a constant flow of gossip items on the living, disclosing who was home on furlough or for convalescence and what news they brought with them of the war and fellow islanders. Microfilms of both newspapers are stored at the Nantucket Atheneum and are accessible to the public.

The archives of the Nantucket Historical Association contain a wealth of fascinating information about Nantucketers who served in the Civil War. They include extensive records of the Nantucket G.A.R., period photographs, letters, medical records, newspaper clippings, scrapbooks, official documents, and dozens of artifacts. Together they help rescue from historical oblivion the *humanity* of many of the otherwise ordinary and forgotten men who filled the ranks of Company I.

Some readers may not be familiar with the Veteran Reserve Corps, in which so many disabled soldiers finished their terms and sometimes reenlisted. To help solve the manpower crises created by the war, Congress created the Invalid Corps. Veterans disabled by wounds or disease resulting from prior service could finish their terms performing guard or hospital duty, thereby releasing able-bodied men for combat. The somewhat demeaning "Invalid Corps" was later changed to Veteran Reserve Corps, and that name is used throughout this roster.

The Civil War Monument is Nantucket's largest public monument. It stands at the head of Main Street, the town's most prestigious avenue, and carved into its granite sides are the names of the seventy-three Nantucket soldiers and sailors who died during the Civil War, including those from the 20th Massachusetts. The generation whose fathers, sons, husbands, and brothers were killed in that conflict was determined that the future not forget them. The annual Memorial Day commemoration observed at the monument is evidence that succeeding generations have not forgotten.

The information contained in a roster such as this is subject to errors of transcription and other inaccuracies introduced by human frailty. The authors apologize for any errors that will inevitably attract the attention of sharp-eyed readers.

Alexander, Edward F., private. Age: 19. Occupation: sailor.

Among the group enlisted and mustered by Lieutenant George Nelson Macy on July 18, 1861.

On September 17, 1862, at the battle of Antietam, he was presumed to have been killed in action. A comrade gave this first-hand account of Alexander's last moments with Company I:

> Private Alexander received a shot in the shoulder, and although advised and even commanded by [Lieutenant Leander F. Alley] to go to the rear, or get in some unexposed position, refused, saying he was not going to leave, but intended to stop and see it through.

He was observed starting for the rear, but he never arrived and his body was never identified or recovered.

His name is on the Civil War monument.

Alley, Leander F., sergeant. Age: 28. Occupation: sailor.

Among the group enlisted and mustered by Lieutenant George Nelson Macy on July 18, 1861, he was the first to sign the roll of volunteers.

On November 1, 1861, after the battle of Ball's Bluff, he was promoted to first sergeant. During the spring 1862 Peninsula Campaign, Alley was described by a comrade:

> Orderly Sergeant Alley is just the man for his place; it is no enviable post to fill, that of a First Sergeant. If any one has any troubles, go to the Orderly; anything wrong, lay it to the Orderly; if our rations are poor, or run short, lay it to the Orderly; so it goes. It is "Alley!" "Alley!" "Alley!" from sunrise to sundown. But Alley always has a word back for all. Then his yarns are so entertaining, that we while away many leisure moments listening with mouth and eyes extended, to some of the most prodigious stories that a person could conveniently imagine. And after closing his toughest yarns, he soberly assures us that every word is true to the letter.

The same comrade observed him under fire and expressed a view widely shared by subordinates and superior officers alike: "Alley [was] on hand whenever there was a chance at a rebel, either with lead or steel—cool as though he was eating a meal at home."

It would be difficult to overstate the regard in which he was held by his comrades. Henry Livermore Abbott, captain of Company I and later the 20th Massachusetts' commanding officer, described Alley in a May 2, 1862, letter to his father: "I have got a stunning first sergeant, a man who has been first mate on a whaler, has made a great deal of money, is thoroughly up in all military knowledge, has always done his duty most faithfully & efficiently & is a devlish smart fellow. . . ." Abbott also described Alley's role in keeping discipline among the ranks: "[Alley] keeps in his tent a long flat stick, known as 'Alley's Spanker,' & when the boys don't behave they catch it."

Alley was promoted to second lieutenant on September 12, 1862, after which the men of Company I contributed money to purchase a presentation sword that is today in the collection of the Nantucket Historical Association.

On December 13, 1862, at the battle of Fredericksburg during an assault on the stone wall at the foot of Marye's Heights, he was killed instantly by a minié ball through his left eye. On Abbott's orders, his body was retrieved under fire by four comrades led by Nantucketer Sergeant John Summerhayes, who later recorded one more sad and gruesome responsibility respecting his former lieutenant:

> [Alley] was well embalmed and would keep for a year at least—his face was dark on one side, owing to the arteries being severed and the blood coagulating. I instructed Private Murphey to have that eye covered with a white Patch which would have concealed the disfigurement. . . . I have lost as true a friend as ever trod the earth.

Abbott personally paid for embalming and transporting the body to Nantucket, selecting Josiah F. Murphey as its escort. On December 27, 1862, the Nantucket *Weekly Mirror* published Alley's obituary:

> **Funeral Obsequies**—The remains of Lieut. Alley arrived here Thursday afternoon, in charge of Private Josiah F. Murphey. On the arrival of the boat at the wharf the body was taken to the hearse, which was draped with the American ensign, and surmounted by a carved gilt eagle. The remains, followed by a long procession, were taken to the residence of his mother, on North Water Street, where they were visited by hundreds of people. There was no attempt at private demonstration beyond the display of flags at half-mast. At two o'clock yesterday afternoon, the body was taken to the North Church, where impressive funeral services were held. After the services the funeral procession formed, and moved to the Unitarian Ground, followed by a large concourse of our citizens. The Public Schools were all closed, and large numbers of our pupils followed the body to its final resting place. The merchants also closed their stores, in respect to the noble dead.

We are permitted to publish the following letter from Capt. Abbot, of Co. I, 20th Regiment Massachusetts Volunteers, to Mrs. Mitchell. Coming from such a source, this letter must be very gratifying to the feelings of the afflicted mother:

'Fredericksburg, Va., Dec. 13, '62

Mrs. Mitchell—**Dear Madame**—Private Josiah F. Murphey, who brings the dead body of your son, will tell you fully all the particulars. I know by judging of my own feelings, how bitterly you will feel his loss. I can say from an intimate acquaintance with him, that he was as brave, resolute and energetic, and at the same time as tender-hearted a man as I ever knew. When I first heard of his death (I didn't see him fall), I felt the same kind of pang as when I first heard of my brother's death, who was killed at Cedar Mountain. It was only a few nights before his death, that he was telling me about his family, and speaking of you in terms of the strongest affection. Every man in the regiment, from the Col. to the men of other companies, respected and admired him as much as any officer that has ever belonged to the regiment. He was a most invaluable officer. A great deal of the superiority of Co. I, to the other companies, is due to Lieut. Alley. I shall never cease to think of him with love, to my dying day. I hope after this bloody war is over, I shall live to express to you, personally, what I have been writing in this letter.

> I remain, my dear madam,
> Yours very respectfully, &c.,
> H.L. Abbott,
> Capt. Co.

Several weeks later, a group of 20th Massachusetts officers would write to Alley's mother and describe her son as having no peer in the regiment in "honesty, energy and decision of character." They continued:

In battle he was wonderfully cool, collected and clear-headed. In the camp he was at once sagacious and indefatigable. His power was immense. He accomplished everything he undertook. No one of his inferiors ever thought for a moment of disobeying him. All his superiors respected him and were always ready to ask his advice. He was unquestionably an invaluable officer.

The letter was signed by, among others, Acting Commander George Nelson Macy; Nathan Hayward, surgeon; Charles W. Folsom, quartermaster; Abbott; future Supreme Court Justice Oliver Wendell Holmes, Jr.; and Lieutenants H.C. Mason, H.L. Patten, and Henry Ropes.

Alley is buried on the south side of Prospect Hill Cemetery on Nantucket and his name appears on the Civil War Monument.

Backus, George Allen, private. Age: 19. Occupation: farmer. Height: 5'7". Hair: light. Comp: fair. Eyes: blue.

Backus enlisted and mustered on August 5, 1862, and joined the regiment at Alexandria on his birthday, August 29. He remained with the regiment until the battle of Cold Harbor in June 1864, where he was severely wounded. Years later, Backus gave this account of his wounding and subsequent abandonment on the Cold Harbor battlefield, a distinction he shared with many other injured and dead comrades that day:

> June 1st I was wounded by a sharpshooter, who grinned at me from a tree. I was shot in the left arm which was broken in two places, as were also three of my ribs. I laid where I fell unconscious for some time, being weak from loss of blood. I was finally found by one of my comrades who carried me to the rear and put me in a hospital. Two surgeons came and examined my wounds and pronounced the one in my side fatal. All right I said, if I am to die, give me something to put me out of my misery. They gave me something to sleep, but it had no effect on me.
>
> The rebs were driving our army back, consequently we had to have our hospital tent moved back to the rear. I was left on a stretcher on the field, to die as they supposed. An ambulance driver coming along, and seeing me, put me into his ambulance, and carried me further back to the rear, where I stayed in the ambulance 4 days. Then I was taken from the ambulance and put into an army wagon and carried to the White House Landing hospital. I stayed there a week and was then carried to the hospital at Alexandria. I remained there two weeks when my term of service having expired, I was sent to Washington where I met my regiment, came home and was discharged. After being home ten months, I went to Dr. Ellis and had the ball extracted from my side, and have it now in my possession as a relic.

The minié ball had entered Backus's left shoulder, fractured the humerus bone, and passed through his rib cage breaking the fifth and sixth ribs before exiting through his chest. Hospitalized at the General Hospital at Fairfax Seminary in Alexandria, Virginia, his arm was "resected" in a reconstructive procedure intended to remove the shattered portion of the bone and join the intact ends. As a result of the operation, his left arm was a half-inch shorter than his right, and badly weakened for life.

He was discharged from hospital shortly before his expiration of service on August 1, 1864.

Backus returned to Nantucket after the war and resumed his former occupation as a farmer. In 1870, he joined the first incarnation of the Nantucket chapter of the G. A. R. He rejoined the G.A.R in 1891 during its island revival.

Private Backus's wound entitled him to pension benefits, and by 1883, they totaled $8 a month. The damage caused by the war followed him to the end of his life. "The fact is," a physician said of him in 1911, "that the man's whole nervous system is a perfect wreck." The doctor attributed Backus's condition to his wartime injuries.

Backus died in Cottage Hospital on Nantucket on February 1, 1917, at the age of 73. The cause of death was listed as arteriosclerosis and pneumonia. He is buried on the north side of Prospect Hill Cemetery in Nantucket.

Backus, Erwin Hinkley, private. Age: 27. Occupation: farmer. Height: 5'6". Hair: brown. Comp: sallow. Eyes: grey.

He enlisted and mustered on July 26, 1862, and was discharged August 1, 1864, by reason of expiration of service. In December 1864, he joined the U. S. Navy and served on various ships including the *Ohio, Hunchback, Vermont, Nyack*, and *Wateree*. He was discharged with the rank of coal heaver in December 1868 by reason of expiration of service.

After his military service, he moved to Napa City, California, where he listed his employment as "manual laborer." For the rest of his life he was afflicted with bronchitis, asthma, and rheumatism, all of which he attributed to his wartime service. The date of his death is unknown.

Baily, George R., private. Age: 18. Occupation: sailor.

He enlisted and mustered on August 8, 1861. On May 31, 1862, he was "bruised" in the ankle from a spent ball at the battle of Fair Oaks. A comrade stated, "Baily finding himself slightly wounded, refused to leave the ranks, until ordered by Lieutenant Abbott."

Between September 17, 1862, and May 3, 1863, he was hospitalized periodically for severe diarrhea. On October 19, 1862, he was discharged from the 20th Massachusetts to enlist in Company C, 4th United States Artillery, a unit of the regular army. On May 3, 1863, he was shot in the left calf at the battle of Chancellorsville, and shortly afterward was admitted to Mount Pleasant Hospital in Washington, D.C. On February 12, 1864, he reenlisted in the regular army and was discharged on February 12, 1867, with the rank of corporal.

After the war he lived in several places working variously as a salesman, bookkeeper, and carpenter. In 1891, an examining physician reported to the pension bureau that Baily suffered from "Rheumatism, disease of heart and legs, chronic diarrhea and gunshot wound to the leg," all of which he attributed to his wartime service. Baily died at the age of 64 on January 19, 1909, from "cardiac dilatation."

Baker, Charles H., private. Age: 18. Occupation: shoe cutter.

He was among the group enlisted and mustered by Lieutenant George Nelson Macy on July 18, 1861. Baker was promoted to corporal on December 23, 1861, and assigned to the Quartermaster Department. He was promoted to quartermaster sergeant on March 10, 1862. Two years later, he reenlisted at Stevensburg, Virginia, and on November 11, 1864, was promoted to first lieutenant of Company C. He was assigned to the Regimental Quartermaster on April 17, 1865, and was promoted to brigade quartermaster on May 25, 1865. On June 2, 1865, he resigned his commission and was honorably discharged.

After the war, he moved to Providence, Rhode Island, married, and worked as a bookkeeper for the Gorham Manufacturing Company, eventually rising to the position of superintendent.

He died in Providence on April 22, 1899, at the age of 55 years, from "angina."

Barnard 2nd, Charles F., private. Age: 22. Occupation: shoemaker. Height: 5'4". Hair: brown. Comp: dark. Eyes: brown.

He was among the group enlisted and mustered by Lieutenant George Nelson Macy on July 18, 1861. After the battle of Ball's Bluff, he was detailed as a hospital steward. On March 1, 1862, he was hospitalized in Poolesville, Maryland, with an undisclosed illness. Unable to march with his regiment when it departed later that month, he was discharged for disability on April 25, 1862.

Barnard reenlisted in Company H of the 13th Veteran Reserve Corps on November 25, 1864, to the credit of Groton, Massachusetts, for which he received a bounty of $325. He was discharged from that unit on November 14, 1865, by reason of expiration of service.

He returned to Nantucket after the war and resumed his occupation as a shoemaker. In July, 1866, a Nantucket physician found he was debilitated with indigestion and pain said to have resulted from being kicked by a horse during the battle at Ball's Bluff.

The designation "2nd" that appears after his name was given to him in the army to differentiate him from another Nantucket recruit with the same name (see below). A comrade stated: "The two Barnards in the Company were known as Barnard 1st and Barnard 2nd, and the Sgt. called the roll in that way."

Another comrade remembered Barnard as "a stout, robust little fellow," who had assisted in rowing the regiment across the Potomac from Harrison's Island to Ball's Bluff. One man remembered him at the time he was discharged for disability: "[Barnard] did not look as though he could live a great while. He had some cough & was very pale."

After the war, he returned to Nantucket and married the sister of his former superior officer, Major Albert B. Holmes. He moved to Brockton, Massachusetts, to continue his trade as a shoemaker. Sick with consumption, he returned to Nantucket two years later and died of the disease on October 12, 1874, at the age of 37. He is buried on Nantucket.

Barnard, Charles F., private. Age: 29. Occupation: sailor. Height: 5'9". Hair: light. Comp: light. Eyes: blue.

He enlisted and mustered on August 19, 1862. On December 13, 1862, he was shot in the head at the battle of Fredericksburg. The injury somehow resulted in "valvular disease of the heart" which, coupled with the effects of chronic diarrhea, resulted in his discharge for disability on August 21, 1863.

He reenlisted in Company A of the 12th Veteran Reserve Corps on November 25, 1864, to the credit of Duxbury, Massachusetts, for which he received a bounty of $325. He was discharged from that unit on November 15, 1865, by reason of expiration of service.

He returned to Nantucket after the war. In June of 1866, a Nantucket physician found that complications from his head wound coupled with "fever & ague," contracted while stationed at Washington, D.C., with the the Veteran Reserve Corps, qualified him for state aid. In 1883 he was receiving a pension of $8 a month.

He died in Sandwich, Massachusetts, on April 24, 1893, and is buried on Nantucket in Prospect Hill Cemetery.

Barnard, Frederick W., private. Age: 21. Occupation: farmer. Height: 6'. Hair: brown. Comp: light. Eyes: grey.

He enlisted and mustered on August 12, 1862, the same day as Josiah Murphey, and joined the regiment on August 29 at Alexandria. Barnard was among those taken sick after the march from Antietam to Harpers Ferry. On October 10, 1862, he was admitted to a hospital there, the first of several that would include stays at facilities in Baltimore and Fairfax Seminary in Virginia.

Years later, Barnard recalled: "The weather was very hot and the march was hard on me coming from this Island [Nantucket] with its bracing sea air." He was diagnosed as having "hypertrophy with chronic Valvulus—disease of the heart" and was discharged for disability on December 31, 1862. He also contracted severe chronic diarrhea which plagued him for the rest of his life.

He returned to Nantucket after discharge and was listed on the town militia list dated July 5, 1864 (required by law to be kept for all males between the ages of 18 and 45) as "home sick."

After the war, he worked as a mariner's mate on the New Bedford, Martha's Vineyard and Nantucket Steamboat Company. In 1889, a pension examiner found that he had "Contracted disease of heart, diarrhea and piles in Sept. 1862 on the march to Antietam and the march back to Harpers Ferry." Franklin Barnard Murphey described him as "a man of few words. . . . When he is through with his work he goes home and behaves himself right until his duties call him forth again."

He died on March 28, 1902, at the age of 61. The cause was "mitral regurgitation," perhaps a result of the heart disease he contracted while in the army.

He is buried in the South Cemetery on Nantucket.

Barnard, John F., private. Age: 22. Occupation: clerk. Height: 6'. Hair: sandy. Comp: fair. Eyes: blue.

He enlisted and mustered on August 12, 1862, the same day as Josiah F. Murphey, and joined the regiment in Alexandria on August 29. He was listed as sick on November 16, 1862, and did not return to duty until April 5, 1863. He was probably among those taken ill after the march from Antietam to Harpers Ferry.

He was promoted to a corporal of Company I sometime in August or July of 1863. In September or October of 1863 he was promoted to sergeant and transferred to Company K. He reenlisted on March 19, 1864, probably in Stevensburg, Virginia. He returned as a sergeant to Company I on July 18, 1864.

He was taken prisoner at the battle of Reams Station on August 25, 1864, and was confined in Libby Prison in Richmond two days later. Sent to Salisbury Prison, North Carolina, he was paroled on October 8, 1864. He died on October 10, 1864, while en route from Belle Isle Prison, probably of disease.

The Nantucket *Weekly Mirror* stated in his obituary: "He was a worthy young man, beloved by all, and his loss will be a severe affliction to his parents. Fountain Engine Co. No. 8 displayed their flag at half-mast on Friday, as a token of respect for their deceased member." His name is on the Civil War Monument.

Barrett, James Henry. private. Age: 17. Occupation: farmer. Height: 5'10". Hair: brown. Comp: dark. Eyes: blue.

Barrett enlisted and mustered on August 14, 1862, and together with Josiah Fitch Murphey joined the regiment in Alexandria on August 29.

While he was advancing up Farquier Street at the battle of Fredericksburg, on December 11, 1862, he was wounded when a spent ball hit his right great toe. Years later, comrade George A. Backus would testify that he heard "[Barrett's] voice crying out in distress" in the field hospital. On December 20, 1862, he was admitted to Carver General Hospital in Washington D.C.

Army surgeons later recommended his transfer to the Veteran Reserve Corps for "hypertrophy of the right great toe," and on November 2, 1863, he transferred to Company A, 6th Veterans Reserve Corps, for his unexpired term of service. He was discharged on July 28, 1864, at its expiration.

He reenlisted in Company I of the 10th Veteran Reserve Corps on December 20, 1864, and mustered out on November 15, 1865, expiration of service.

Barrett was in Washington when Lincoln was assassinated and was one of those detailed to guard Secretary of State William H. Seward after he had been savagely knifed in the face by one of the Booth conspirators. Later, Barrett was assigned to guard Mrs. Surratt, Lewis Paine, and Dr. Samuel Mudd, all accused of conspiring to kill Lincoln. Many years later, he recalled:

It was a mighty critical time. The people were pretty nearly crazy with grief and anger over Lincoln's death, and they crowded around the prison all day and all night. It's a good thing the army was still in the capital.

I was one of the guards around the cells. I can remember those prisoners' faces as if I saw them yesterday. Payne [sic] was only a young chap, and looked scared to death. Mrs. Surratt was a very beautiful woman, dark and with white skin and dark eyes. Dr. Mudd was a pitiful figure, and most of us felt sorry for him, although none dared let on how he felt.

We kept a close guard. The prisoners weren't allowed to whisper to each other. Had to talk aloud when they had anything to say. We had strict orders to listen carefully to whatever they said, and to report it as quickly as possible afterwards. Yes, that was an exciting time.

Did I ever see Lincoln? Yes, many times on Pennsylvania Avenue, where I was stationed. He did not look like a President, more like a farmer, but all the soldiers who knew him swore by him."

In an article published in the Nantucket *Journal* in 1893, Barrett recalled meeting Lincoln while the latter visited soldiers in Carney Hospital in Washington, where Barrett was still recovering from his Fredericksburg wound. Barrett wrote: "While I was [in Carney] President Lincoln came through the hospital, the first time I had ever seen him. So I went up to him and he gave me a hearty shake of the hand."

Barrett returned to Nantucket following the war and married Mary H. Backus, whose first husband, Charles H. Backus, had served with the 2nd Massachusetts Cavalry and had been killed at the battle of Cedar Creek in 1862. Barrett lived for a time in New Bedford, Massachusetts, and worked as a "night fireman" at a large mill. Through the years he received various pensions for "rheumatism in the right foot." He eventually returned to Nantucket and joined the local G. A. R. chapter in 1870, giving his occupation as a "laborer." He renewed his membership in 1892 during the island revival of the G. A. R.

His long life, congenial temperament, and identification with Civil War veterans affairs assured him a place of stature in the Nantucket community. After the revival of the Nantucket G. A. R., Barrett became a fixture at Memorial Day commemorations. Beginning in 1906, Barrett was among those Civil War veterans who paid annual visits to the public schools to share stories of their wartime experiences. In his later years, columns of Nantucket schoolchildren would parade by his house as part of the Memorial Day Commemoration. He remained a lifelong friend of Josiah Fitch Murphey.

He died on Nantucket on June 21, 1938, at the age of 93 from "acute obstruction of urinary bladder," and was the second of the last three surviving Nantucket Civil War veterans.

Barrett, William H., private. Age: 18. Occupation: farmer. Height: 5'4 1/2". Hair: black. Comp: dark. Eyes: brown.

He was among those enlisted and mustered by Lieutenant George Nelson Macy on July 18, 1861. Barrett was briefly a corporal—from November 1862 to February 1863—and on February 20, 1863, was reduced to the ranks for undisclosed reasons. Taken prisoner at the battle of Gettysburg, July 3, 1863, he was paroled at Annapolis, Maryland, in September or October. He was discharged on August 1, 1864, by reason of expiration of service.

After the war he moved to San Diego, California. He died there on Christmas Day 1906, at the age of 63.

Barrett, William Alexander, private. Age: 18. Occupation: fisherman. Height: 5'5". Hair: dark. Comp: fair. Eyes: black.

He enlisted and mustered the same day as Josiah F. Murphey on August 12, 1862, and joined the regiment at Alexandria on August 29. On March 1, 1863, he was discharged at Camp Banks, Virginia, for "organic disease of the heart, so affected after enlisting." On December 15, 1863, he enlisted and mustered in Company F of the 2nd Massachusetts Cavalry and received a bounty of $325. While serving with that unit, he was shot in the left leg at the battle of Cedar Creek and taken prisoner. From August 12, 1864, to June 1865, he was a prisoner at the Confederate prison in Danville, Virginia. After his release, he was hospitalized at Alexandria for severe diarrhea and malaria contracted in prison. He was discharged for disability on July 7, 1865.

Barrett returned to Nantucket after the war and was employed as a farmer and laborer, but he was permanently disabled by disease. Two friends testified about him:

> We have witnessed the attacks of chills followed by fever. The attacks leave him weak, and he complains of pain in the limbs. . . . We have seen evidences of diarrhea, in summer more than in the winter, but in both summer & winter he has been troubled with it, and has with the malarial poisoning been greatly weakened thereby. The evidences are his frequently going to stool.

He joined the Nantucket chapter of the G. A. R. during its island revival in 1891.

He died in August 1923.

Bunker, William R., private. Age: 18. Occupation: shoemaker.

He enlisted and mustered on August 2, 1861. In June 1863, he transferred to Company A of the 3rd Veteran Reserve Corps and was discharged on August 1, 1864, probably for expiration of service.

After the war, he lived in Brockton, Massachusetts, but eventually returned to Nantucket. He joined the Nantucket chapter of the G. A. R. in its first incarnation in 1867.

He is buried in South Cemetery in Nantucket.

Cartwright, Edmund G.W., corporal. Age: 18. Occupation: scholar. Height: 5'10 1/2". Hair: brown. Comp: dark. Eyes: blue.

He was among those enlisted and mustered by Lieutenant George Nelson Macy on July 18, 1861. On June 20, 1862, at the battle of Nelson's Farm, Virginia, he was wounded by a piece of shell and then struck by an artillery wagon. He was hospitalized in Washington, D.C., from July to December 1862.

In January 1863, he volunteered for "special duty" to accept an officer's commission with newly appointed Brigadier General Daniel Ullman, who was recruiting a colored brigade in Louisiana. On February 2, 1863, he was detached as a first lieutenant to serve with Company G of the 9th Regiment of the Corps d'Afrique, whose name was subsequently changed to the 81st Regiment United States Colored Troops.

In June 1863, during the siege of Port Hudson, Louisiana, his horse fell and he was hospitalized for injuries. Sometime during his Louisiana service he contracted malaria. He was to suffer intermittent chills and fever for the rest of his life. His military doctor recommended a change in climate, and on September 8, 1864, he was discharged to enlist in the 3rd Massachusetts Heavy Artillery stationed in Washington, D.C. On November 16 he was again promoted to first lieutenant to head Company A of that regiment. He was discharged September 18, 1865, for expiration of service.

After the war, he settled in Haverhill, Massachusetts, and worked as a bookkeeper. He died on June 7, 1886, at the age of 43, from "malaria and marasmus."

Cathcart, James F., private. Age: 38. Occupation: seaman on a whaling vessel; served on "3 or 4" whaling voyages before the war.

Height: 5'4 1/2". Hair: brown. Comp: light. Eyes: grey.

He enlisted and mustered the same day as Josiah F. Murphey on August 12, 1862, and joined the regiment at Alexandria on August 29. Cathcart was among those who fell ill after the march from Antietam to Harpers Ferry, suffering from severe diarrhea. Nonetheless, he remained with the regiment until after the battle of Fredericksburg, in December 1862.

On December 27, 1862, he was admitted to the regimental hospital for a "disease of the lungs" before being transferred to the hospital steamer *Mary Washington* and taken to Finley General Hospital in Washington, D.C., where he was admitted on December 29, 1862, for "general debility." He was discharged for disability on March 14, 1863, for lung disease.

In 1879, a physician described him as "A small feeble man. . . . The intercostal muscles of the back appear to be affected with Rheumatism at this time. . . . He is unable to perform any hard labor."

In 1892, in depositions submitted to support the pension claim of his widow, no less than seven of his former comrades, all but one of whom were Nantucketers, testified to the physical debilities brought on by the Harpers Ferry march. Josiah F. Murphey stated:

> [After Antietam] we marched to Harpers Ferry where we forded the Potomac River and went in to camp on Boliver Heights, wet and tired on that night[.] [W]e suffered terribly. [T]here was a cold wind but we were in our wet clothing and no blankets or wood to build fires and all of us suffered greatly and many of the men took cold and had chills and fever[,] rheumatism and diarrhea and some had Typhoid fever and died there. It was very severe on the new recruits.

Cathcart died on January 16, 1892 of "rheumatism" and "La Grippe" (influenza). He is buried on the north side of Prospect Hill Cemetery in Nantucket.

Chadwick, George W., private. Age: 19. Occupation: shoemaker. Height: 5'10". Hair: brown. Comp: fair. Eyes: blue.

He enlisted and mustered the same day as Josiah F. Murphey on August 12, 1862. Following the march to Harpers Ferry after the battle of Antietam, he contracted dysentery and on November 26 was admitted to Camp A United States General Hospital in Frederick, Maryland. Although dysentery is a wasting disease, and his doctors were doubtless aware of his true condition, Chadwick was somehow induced to send the following letter:

"U.S. Gen. Hospital,
Near Frederick Md. Jan. 14. 1863.

Dear Father:

I feel greatly encouraged this morning the doctor has just been to see me and he says that I will get along very well and as soon as I am able he will discharge me and send me home.

He tells me to be cheerful and lively and to not get downhearted. Nothing would please me so much as to get a discharge and come home where I can have the care of loved ones. It is a hard thing to be cheerful here, where all are so outragious. Yet I receive much kind attention from others in the tent.

I will now close hoping to hear from you soon, and may God Bless you.

My love to you all.
Remember me to all friends.
Your affectionate
son Geo. W. Chadwick
Direct as formerly.

P.S. If any of you could conveniently come down here I would be glad to see you. If you can, come to Frederick City Maryland then to Camp A, Ward D. No. 8

George.

[P.S.S.] I got my friend Jas. M. Philips to write for me for it tires me to write much. I hope soon to be able to write myself.

Chadwick died the next day.

Chase, Daniel B., private. Age: 42. Occupation: mason. Height: 5'5", Hair: brown. Comp: light. Eyes: blue.

He enlisted and mustered the same day as Josiah F. Murphey on August 12, 1862, and joined the regiment at Alexandria on August 29. On December 11, 1862, at the battle of Fredericksburg, he was shot in the leg and hand. On July 3, 1863, at the battle of Gettysburg, he was wounded again by a bullet in his left hand while defending against Pickett's Charge. At a field hospital at Gettysburg his middle finger was amputated from the second joint.

Chase was transferred to the Chestnut Street Hospital in Philadel-phia, Pennsylvania, where he remained four and a half months. On January 10, 1864, he transferred to the 134th Company, 2nd Bat-talion Veteran Reserve Corps and resided at the Cliffburne Barracks in Washington, D. C. During that service, he performed hospital duty and was discharged on November 10, 1864.

Chase returned to Nantucket after the war and in 1868 joined the Nantucket chapter of the G. A. R. in its first incarnation.

He died on Nantucket from "heart failure" on February 12, 1900, at the age of 78. He is buried on the south side of Prospect Hill Ceme-tery on Nantucket.

Christian, Samuel, private. Age: 29. Occupation: farmer. Height: 5'4". Hair: brown. Comp: dark. Eyes: blue.

He enlisted and mustered the same day as Josiah F. Murphey on August 12, 1862, and joined the regiment at Alexandria on August 29. He was absent sick after October 30, 1862, and was probably one of those taken ill after the march from Antietam to Harpers Ferry. He finally returned to duty on March 28, 1863.

On July 3, 1863, at the battle of Gettysburg, he was wounded while defending against Pickett's Charge. The location and severity of the wound is not disclosed, but probably as a result he was detached to division headquarters as a provost guard, considered light duty. He is mentioned by Murphey as one of those detailed to act as a "sec-ond" in the execution of an unnamed deserter.

On May 18, 1864, at the battle of Spotsylvania Court House, Chris-tian was severely wounded. According to the testimony of a com-rade, he was left for dead on the battlefield. An army physician described the wound as follows:

[A] ball from a minie rifle entering the left side of the neck about two inches below the lobe of the ear, passed in a downward direction through the neck and right shoulder shattering the glenoid cavity and head and neck of the humerus—resection has been per-formed—six inches of the humerus and glenoid cavity of the scapula removed—arm entirely useless—left side practically paralyzed[,] almost entire loss of sensation in arm and leg (the ball passed behind the spinal chord).

Although he was discharged on August 1, 1864, due to the expiration of service, he was unable to travel and remained at Emory General Hospital in Washington, D.C., until January 30, 1865. At release, he was rated permanently and totally disabled. He received a pension of $8 per month.

In 1867, a physician declared that his Spotsylvania wound was not yet fully healed. Various doctors noted his chronic pain resulting from the wound, and one year before his death Dr. J. B. King of Nantucket reported that "[Christian's] neuralgic pain compels him to keep morphine constantly on hand."

Christian returned to Nantucket after the war, and in spite of his injuries served successfully as town clerk until his death on July 19, 1875, at the age of 42. He is buried on the south side of Prospect Hill Cemetery on Nantucket.

Coffin, Albert C., private. Age: 22. Occupation: grocery delivery boy. Height: 5'5". Hair: brown. Comp: fair. Eyes: blue.

He enlisted and mustered on July 26, 1862, and was among those who fell ill after the march from Antietam to Harpers Ferry. He became "sick with Chronic diarrhea and physically prostrated while on pickett duty," and shortly thereafter was stricken with typhoid fever. Others remembered Coffin collapsing on the march itself, and how Lieutenant Albert B. Holmes and Sergeant Leander F. Alley "carried his gun, cartridge box and knapsack to enable him to keep up on the march." Whenever his physical breakdown occurred, on December 21, 1862, he was admitted to Fort Schuyler Hospital and was discharged from the army for disability on January 1, 1863.

On June 24, 1863, he reenlisted in Company H of the 2nd Veteran Reserve Corps, in which he guarded Confederate prisoners at Fort Monroe, Virginia. He was discharged for disability from the V.R.C. on August 11, 1864, probably for severe diarrhea.

Coffin returned to Nantucket after the war. By 1878, he was rated totally disabled from "chronic diarrhea and general debility." Dr. J. B. King of Nantucket described him at that time: "[Coffin] is a feeble looking man, somewhat emaciated, red tongue, dilated pupils, hard of hearing, and all together a used up looking man. He states that he is laid up much of the time with diarrhea, and is at all times unable to labor."

By 1883, he was receiving a pension of $12 per month for "chronic diarrhea," and in 1891 joined the Nantucket chapter of the G. A. R. during its revival. By this time, however, Coffin was far more seriously ill than he had ever been. Neighbors described him as "a wreck of the former man they knew him to be."

On August 16, 1894, Albert Coffin was judged legally insane and a guardian was appointed by the court. Coffin died on March 19, 1903, and is buried on the south side of Prospect Hill Cemetery on Nantucket.

Coffin, George H., private. Age: 17. Occupation: miller. Height: 5'6". Hair: brown. Comp: light. Eyes: blue.

He enlisted and mustered on August 14, 1862, and joined the regiment at Alexandria on August 29. On December 11, 1862, at the battle of Fredericksburg, he was wounded by a bullet in the right shoulder, ". . . resulting in rigidity of joint and which renders him unfit for military service."

He was hospitalized at Finley General Hospital, Washington, D.C., and on January 19, 1863, was discharged for disability. One year later he enlisted as a private in the 2nd Massachusetts Cavalry, receiving a bonus of $325. On May 2, 1864, he transferred to the Navy and served on the USS *Saratoga* and *Macedonian*. He died on August 28, 1865, from unknown causes while serving as an ordinary seaman on board the USS *Ohio*.

His name is on the Civil War Monument.

Conway, Patrick, private. Age: probably 38. Occupation: laborer. Born in Clare, Ireland. Height: 5'8". Hair: Black. Comp: dark. Eyes: grey.

He was among the group enlisted and mustered by Lieutenant George Nelson Macy on July 18, 1861. Conway served as company cook.

On July 1, 1862, at the battle of Malvern Hill, Virginia, he was shot by two buckshot in the right leg. One ball was removed, and the other remained in him for life. Shortly afterward, while raising a tent at Harrison's Landing, Virginia, he was seriously injured when it collapsed and a tent pole struck him on the spine. He was sent to Craney Island Hospital, near Fort Monroe, Virginia, on August 16. He returned to duty on April 6, 1863, and was mustered out of duty on August 1, 1864, by reason of expiration of service.

He returned to Nantucket after the war, plagued by his wartime injuries. In August of 1866, he was diagnosed with severe rheumatism in his "left arm particularly." From 1869 onward, he was consistently rated at "one-half" capacity to support himself. In an 1872 application for pension benefits his physician noted "He is an honest patient [and an] ignorant sufferer, and served his time out as a soldier, teamster, or whatever he was told to do."

But the war had taken its toll. Toward the end of his life, an especially unsympathetic physician noted, "The man drinks and takes no special care of himself and I have no doubt all of these symptoms are aggravated by his mode of life." As of 1883, he received a pension of $4 per month.

He died on Nantucket on September 12, 1889, at the age of 66. He is buried in the Roman Catholic Cemetery on Nantucket.

Cook, Henry P., company or regimental cook. Age: 34. Occupation: sailor; employed in laying underwater cable before the war. Born in Newburyport, Massachusetts. Illiterate. Height: 5'8". Hair: brown. Comp: dark. Eyes: hazel.

He was among those enlisted and mustered by Lieutenant George Nelson Macy on July 18, 1861. A comrade described the reasons for which Cook was later assigned light duty as a hospital steward and before that, in December 1861, assigned as a cook: ". . . while on the march from Washington, D. C. to Poolesville, Maryland, in September 1861, [Cook] contracted varicose veins and ulcers in the left leg. . . . He was detailed to the Gen. Hospital near Yorktown and did not again join the company."

On April 30, 1862, he was finally detached as a hospital steward to a general hospital near Yorktown, Virginia, and several months later transferred in that capacity to the hospital steamer *State of Maine*. On July 2 he suffered a severe sunstroke while the ship was anchored near Harrison's Landing, Virginia, and was hospitalized at Dunbarton Street Hospital, Georgetown, D. C.

On January 5, 1863, he was discharged for disability. His army physician gave the following reason:

> Great nervous debility consequent on sun stroke amounting, under any unusual excitement, or exertion, to syncope (loss of consciousness due to inadequate blood flow to the brain). I also found a glandular enlargement in the Politeal space, which materially interferes with walking. Contracted since enlistment.

Cook returned to Nantucket after the war, and as of 1883 received a pension of $6 per month. Sometime later he moved to Maine and remained incapacitated with "headaches, dizziness and poor sleep" for the rest of his life.

He died in Augusta, Maine, on September 4, 1900, at the age of 72.

Cottle, Freeman R., private. Age: 21. Occupation: seaman. Height: 5' 3 1/2". Hair: brown. Comp: dark. Eyes: blue.

He enlisted and mustered the same day as Josiah F. Murphey, on August 12, 1862, and joined the regiment at Alexandria on August 29. On December 13, 1862, Cottle was one of the four men who, under constant fire, retrieved Alley's body from the stone wall at the Battle of Fredericksburg. In September or October 1863, Cottle was promoted to corporal, and afterward was a color bearer for the regiment.

He reenlisted on December 20, 1863, and received a $325 bounty. On April 7, 1864, he swore on oath that before the war he had served in the merchant service since 1854, and on April 21 he was permitted to transfer to the U. S. Navy. He served with the rank of ordinary seaman and coxswain on the USS *North Carolina* and USS *Bienville*. He was discharged from the Navy on April 24, 1865.

After the war he moved to Cottage City (Oak Bluffs), Martha's Vineyard, and his occupation was listed as "engineer." Later, he was granted a pension for deafness and rheumatism, both of which were attributed to wartime service. He died of pneumonia on January 19, 1906.

Crocker, Samuel C., private. Age: 18. Occupation: farmer. Height: 5'9". Hair: dark. Comp: dark. Eyes: hazel.

He enlisted and mustered the same day as Josiah F. Murphey, on August 12, 1862. Crocker was later promoted to corporal, date and place unknown. On May 3, 1863, at the battle of Chancellorsville, he shot off the forefinger of his left hand when his musket accidentally discharged. On May 6, 1863, he was sent to the Mount Pleasant General Hospital in Washington, D. C., where the stump of his finger was amputated at the second joint. He was released on June 4, 1863, and returned to Company I.

On May 12, 1864, at the battle of Spotsylvania, he was shot in the lower lip, but was not hospitalized. On August 25, 1864, at the battle of Reams Station, Virginia, he was taken prisoner, and on August 29, was sent to Libby Prison in Richmond. On October 9 he was transferred to the prisoner-of-war camp at Salisbury, North Carolina. Sometime afterward, he was admitted to the prison hospital and died there on January 31, 1865, of pneumonia.

The Nantucket *Weekly Mirror* stated in his obituary:

> Private Crocker was also quite a young man, and of an unusually hardy and robust nature; he was a true and tried soldier, and had been with the 20th regiment throughout all the terrible trials to which that regiment had been exposed, and had been twice wounded. He also was taken prisoner at Reams' Station, and the cruel and barbarous treatment to which he was exposed, finally wore him out, and he died on the 30th of January [*sic*] last. His loss will be a severe blow to his parents, and a large family of younger brothers and sisters.

His name is on the Civil War Monument. His body was returned and is buried in the New North Cemetery on Nantucket.

Crocker, Charles M., private/drummer. Age: 18. Occupation: farmer. Height: 5' 3 1/2". Hair: dark. Comp: dark. Eyes: black.

He enlisted and mustered on February 29, 1864, and was marked "Passed for a Musician" by Dr. A. B. Hall, examining surgeon. He was to remain a drummer throughout his service. On March 18, Crocker joined the regiment at Stevensburg, Virginia.

Crocker fought with the regiment throughout the spring of 1864. Sometime after the battle of Cold Harbor, he was diagnosed with rheumatism and catarrh. These symptoms foreshadowed the malaria from which he suffered for the rest of his life.

He was discharged on July 16, 1865, by reason of expiration of service. He returned to Nantucket after the war, married, and had one child. In 1891, he joined the Nantucket chapter of the G. A. R. during its island revival, giving his occupation as a "laborer."

Crocker died on November 20, 1927, at the Nantucket Cottage Hospital and is buried in New North Cemetery on Nantucket.

Depung, Caleb Lyons, private. Age: 34. Occupation: farmer. Height: 5'5 1/2". Hair: dark. Comp: sallow. Eyes: blue.

He enlisted on July 16, 1862, and mustered on July 22. On October 19 he became ill with "bleeding from the lungs," and was sent to a military hospital in Frederick, Maryland, another casualty of the march between Antietam and Harpers Ferry.

Nantucketer Albert B. Holmes, his sergeant and later major in the regiment, stated:

> [Depung] took part with us in the battle of Antietam, marched from there to Harpers Ferry, fording the Potomac River on our way. At Harpers Ferry soon after our arrival, he was taken sick which appeared to be the result of fatigue and exposure and went from there into hospital.

Josiah F. Murphey stated that after Antietam and the march to Harpers Ferry, "[Depung] told me that the army service was using him up." Another Nantucket comrade, Alvin Hull, remembered Depung as a "stout robust man and in excellent health . . . until [the] march to Harpers Ferry.

In October 1863, Depung transferred to Company D of the 6th Veteran Reserve Corps. On January 15, 1864, he died from pneumonia at the U.S. General Hospital at Armory Square in Washington, D. C. His name is on the Civil War Monument.

Ellis, Charles F., private. Age: 20. Occupation: farmer. Height: 5'8". Hair: black. Comp: dark. Eyes: black.

He enlisted and mustered the same day as Josiah F. Murphey, on August 12, 1862. On December 11, 1862, at the battle of Fredericksburg, he was shot in the left ankle by a bullet lodging deep in the bone. Hospitalized for seventeen days in a field hospital, on December 28, 1862, he was transferred to Douglas Hospital in Washington, D. C. There his left foot was amputated.

Dr. John E. Smith, acting assistant surgeon, noted after the amputation that Ellis was "in good spirits—appetite good and manifest improvement constitutionally." He was prescribed a diet of egg nog, beef tea, and chicken soup. Soon, however, Dr. Smith noted on Ellis's record: "Patient does not seem so well—Fever—pulse 120. . . . Clear case of hospital gangrene in my opinion others do not agree with me. Patient sinking rapidly—at night died." The final notation was on January 19, 1863.

Ellis is buried in Prospect Hill Cemetery on Nantucket and his name is on the Civil War Monument.

Ellis, Andrew S., private. Age: 27. Occupation: carpenter. Height: 5' 4". Hair: black. Comp: dark. Eyes: black.

He enlisted and mustered August 14, 1862, and joined the regiment at Alexandria on August 29. He was among those who fell ill following the march from Antietam to Harpers Ferry. He was discharged for disability on December 24, 1863, in part for a growing paralysis on his left side that was attributed to the hardships of the march.

After the war, he moved to South Abington, Massachusetts, and worked as a shoemaker, but due to his physical infirmities, became destitute, and was eventually supported by the local chapter of the G. A. R. He died in Whitman, Massachusetts, on December 23, 1891, at the age of 58 from "disease of the lungs."

Enos, John B., private. Age: 27. Occupation: farmer. Height: 5' 4". Hair: dark. Comp: dark. Eyes: blue.

He enlisted and mustered on August 19, 1862, and joined the regiment at Rockville, Maryland, on September 4. During the months of November and December he served as a hospital nurse. In April 1863 he became ill and was absent from the regiment until his transfer to Company E, 9th Veteran Reserve Corps, on October 2, 1863.

He was discharged from the Veteran Reserve Corps on July 26, 1864, for expiration of service, and then on March 17, 1865, enlisted in the U. S. Navy as an ordinary seaman serving with the North Atlantic Squadron. He was discharged as a seaman at Portsmouth, New Hampshire, on February 3, 1868, because of expiration of service.

He returned to Nantucket after his naval service and joined the Nantucket chapter of the G. A. R. during its island revival in 1891. He is buried on the south side of Prospect Hill Cemetery on Nantucket.

Farnham, Henry Clay, private. Age: 35. Occupation: boot maker. Height: 6' 1 1/2". Hair: light. Comp: fair. Eyes: blue.

He enlisted and mustered the same day as Josiah F. Murphey, August 12, 1862, and joined the regiment at Alexandria on August 29. He is reported to have been wounded at Antietam, ". . . knocked down by a spent ball." He was wounded again in 1863, day and place unknown. On August 1, 1864, he was discharged by expiration of service.

After the war, Farnham moved to Sandwich, Massachusetts, and later, New Bedford, where at the time of his death he was employed as the janitor of a bank. He died from a cerebral hemorrhage on September 2, 1907, at the age of 70.

Fisher, Hiram, private. Age: 42. Occupation: fisherman and blacksmith. Height: 5'9 1/2". Hair: grey. Comp: light. Eyes: blue.

The father of soldier Charles H. Fisher (see below), he enlisted August 14, 1862, and mustered on August 19. He was actually forty-eight years old at enlistment, and no doubt falsified his age to avoid the forty-five-year age limit.

Fisher was discharged for disability on February 3, 1864, diagnosed with "paralysis agitans" and assessed by army physicians as "able to earn his subsistance in part" but "Unfit for Invalid Corps—disability one (1/3) third."

Eight months after Hiram's discharge, he and Charles drowned together when their sailboat capsized in a gale between Nantucket and Tuckernuck Island, where the two men had gone to visit friends. Ironically, it was near the same spot where Hiram's father, Captain Meltiah Fisher, had drowned in a similar accident many years before. Hiram is buried in Old North Cemetery on Nantucket.

Fisher, Charles H., private. Age: 18. Occupation: fisherman. Height: 5' 5 1/2". Hair: brown. Comp: light. Eyes: grey.

The son of Hiram Fisher (see above), he enlisted and mustered February 29, 1864. A rejected recruit, he was discharged for disability for undisclosed reasons on April 25, 1864.

Charles drowned with his father when their sailboat capsized. When his body was recovered three weeks later, one of his arms was "tightly holding the lifeless body of a small dog." He is buried in Old North Cemetery on Nantucket.

Folger, Henry S., private. Age: 34. Occupation: farmer. Height: 5' 6". Hair: light. Comp: light. Eyes: blue.

He enlisted on August 14, 1862, and mustered on August 19. He was discharged on August 1, 1864, expiration of service. His name is on the Civil War Monument, although no record of service-related death has been found.

Folger, Reuben S., private. Age: 38. Occupation: seaman. Height: 5' 5 1/4". Hair: black. Comp: dark. Eyes: blue.

He enlisted and mustered the same day as Josiah F. Murphey on August 12, 1862. On June 24, 1863, he was discharged for disability at Fort Wood in New York Harbor for "Disease of mitral valves and epistaxis, both existing before enlistment."

He reenlisted in Company E, 2nd Massachusetts Volunteer Heavy Artillery on September 27, 1863. He was discharged on May 18, 1864, enlisted in the U. S. Navy, and served in the Gulf Squadron on board the USS *Minnesota*.

He returned to Nantucket after his naval service and gave his occupation as laborer. In August of 1866 he was examined by a Nantucket physician who noted he had been discharged for a "nosebleed" and other unspecified disabilities, which included a bout of temporary blindness contracted after the battle of Antietam. At the time of the examination, the doctor concluded that Folger continued to suffer from "Epistaxis at times—[he] has it now & is debilitated & unable to labor much of the time." He joined the Nantucket chapter of the G. A. R. during its revival in 1891.

Folger died on June 23, 1903, from "senility" at the age of 79. He is buried in South Cemetery on Nantucket.

Fuller, Henry G., private. Age: 27. Occupation: seaman.

One of the few draftees from Nantucket, he mustered into the 19th Massachusetts Volunteer Infantry on July 13, 1863. In January 1864 he transferred to Company I of the 20th Massachusetts.

By spring 1864, Pvt. Fuller had apparently concluded that life would be easier on the main. On April 7 he appeared before Captain Arthur Curtis and Lieutenant Henry Bond of Company I and swore under oath that he had "served in the whaling service nine (9) years and in the merchant service three (3) years, since the year 1851," and requested a transfer to the U. S. Navy. His request was granted on April 21.

Fuller served on board the USS *Chicopee*, but on May 19, two weeks after reporting for duty, he may have concluded that life elsewhere would be easier than life on the main, and he deserted. He has no further record.

Greene, Edward P., private. Age: 21. Occupation: clerk.

He was among the group enlisted and mustered by Lieutenant George Nelson Macy on July 18, 1861. On April 6, 1862, at Big Bethel, Maryland, he deserted, but returned to the regiment on August 4, 1862.

On December 11, 1862, at the battle of Fredericksburg, Virginia, he was wounded in the arm. In March or April of 1863, he was promoted to corporal. He deserted again at the battle of Gettysburg on July 3, 1863, but returned to the regiment on August 10, 1863. Punishment, if any, for either instance of desertion, is undisclosed.

On May 12, 1864, at the battle of Spotsylvania, he was wounded by a minié ball in the little finger, and on May 28, 1864, was admitted to Mount Pleasant General Hospital, Washington, D.C. He was discharged on August 1, 1864, by reason of expiration of service.

Holmes, Albert B., private. Age: 19. Occupation: sailor. Height: 5'5 1/2". Hair: dark. Comp: dark. Eyes: black.

He was among those enlisted and mustered by Lieutenant George Nelson Macy on July 18, 1861. Promoted to corporal after Ball's Bluff, he advanced to sergeant on February 5, 1862, and first sergeant on April 29. He was promoted to second lieutenant on October 19, 1863.

He was described by a comrade as one of the "neatest men among us—always on hand when wanted." Wounded slightly in the hand at the battle of Fredericksburg, he was promoted to first lieutenant just after Gettysburg and to captain of Company A on March 21, 1864.

Holmes was wounded in action on May 6, 1864, during the Wilderness Campaign when he was shot through the right lung. On November 4, 1864, he was ordered discharged for disability, but refused, and was soon reinstated to command by his friend and fellow islander George Nelson Macy, by then a colonel. On October 31 he was placed in temporary command of the 20th Massachusetts.

He served as an inspector on the brigade staff of General William A. Olmstead. Although mustered out as captain of Company A, he received a brevet appointment to major of United States Volunteers to date March 13, 1865, "for conspicuous gallantry at the battle of Armstrong's Mills." He mustered out July 16, 1865.

He returned to Nantucket after the war and joined the local chapter of the G.A.R. in 1867 during its first incarnation. That year, he was examined by a Nantucket physician and was found to be ". . .

unable to labor. [He] has cough and purulent expectoration if much exertion is used." He served as customs collector for the district of Nantucket from July 31, 1875, to 1883.

Afterward, he moved to his wife's home in Livermore Falls, Maine, and spent the rest of his career as an executive with the International Paper Company. Pensioned after the war at $20 per month, he died of heart disease at the age of 76 on March 19, 1919, and is buried in Livermore Falls.

Hull, Alvin, private. Age: 18. Occupation: fisherman. Height: 5' 3". Hair: light. Comp: light. Eyes: blue.

He enlisted and mustered on August 19, 1862, and joined the regiment on September 4. He was among those who fell ill after the march from Antietam to Harpers Ferry and recalled the circumstances years later:

> [I] was disabled from service [as I] suffered from exposure in crossing the river Potomac and sleeping on the damp of the river bank. [I] suppose that the disease was Typhoid fever, but [have] no distinct recollection of disability being delerious a portion of the time.

On October 7, 1863, Hull was transferred to the Veteran Reserve Corps and, ultimately, to Company D of the 20th Veteran Reserve Corps, on February 6, 1864. He was discharged on August 1, 1864, by reason of expiration of service.

He returned to Nantucket after the war but never enjoyed his prewar health. Fit only for "light labor," he worked as a janitor, a messenger, and finally, as town crier for the Town of Nantucket.

He died from a cerebral hemorrhage on August 10, 1906, and is buried in the Soldiers' Lot in Prospect Hill Cemetery on Nantucket.

Hunter, Jared M., private. Age: 18. Occupation: farmer.

He was among those enlisted and mustered by Lieutenant George Nelson Macy on July 18, 1861. On June 30, 1862, he was killed in action at the Battle of Nelson's Farm, Virginia. A comrade furnished this account of his last moments:

> He was struck by a rifle ball, killing him instantly, while loading and firing on the

enemy; not a sound escaped his lips. He fell as many others did that day, in performance of his duty. A few moments before, his voice was as loud and strong as any among us. Little did he imagine then that he had but an hour to stay with us.

In fact, the bullet that killed Private Hunter had already passed through the neck of the man in front of him.

His name is on the Civil War Monument.

Jones, Henry, private. Age: 18. Occupation: farmer. Height: 5' 10". Hair: fair. Comp: fair. Eyes: light.

He enlisted and mustered on July 19, 1862, and joined the regiment at Harrison's Landing on August 4. From December 31, 1862, until his return on April 26, 1863, he was absent without leave. No action appears to have been taken against him. On July 3, 1863, he was mortally wounded at the battle of Gettysburg defending against Pickett's Charge.

Shortly after Jones died, Captain Henry Livermore Abbott wrote to Asa P. Jones, the soldier's father:

> Notwithstanding his apparent feebleness, he stood all the hardships of the march with great pluck, never falling out. And it is sufficient testimony to his gallantry in action, to state that his body was found by the clump of trees, where the battle was fiercest, and within a few rods of the rebel lines. Believe me, that I sympathize most deeply with you in the loss of so young and gallant a boy.

Jones was still alive when found, shot through the head. He died at a field hospital on July 4.

Kelley, William P., private. Age: 18. Occupation: scholar. Height: 5'7 1/2". Hair: dark. Comp: fair. Eyes: blue.

He was among those enlisted and mustered by Lieutenant George Nelson Macy on July 18, 1861. The excellent physical condition of the Nantucket recruits generally was noted by several observers, but Kelley surpassed them all. Regimental historian George A. Bruce commented: "Those present [at the induction of the Nantucketers] will never forget Surgeon Bryant's delight at the physique of the Nantucket recruits, especially that of Sergeant Kelly [*sic*] when he removed his clothes."

Kelley was promoted to corporal on November 11, 1861. On May 31, 1862, at the battle of Fair Oaks, he received a "flesh wound of the leg" and was admitted to hospital on June 1. On September 5, 1862, he was promoted to first sergeant. On March 22, 1864 he reenlisted at Stevensburg, Virginia.

Josiah F. Murphey witnessed Kelley's capture by the Confederates on May 12, 1864, at the battle of Spotsylvania. He was sent to the prison camp at Salisbury, North Carolina.

On February 26, 1865, he was paroled at N.E. Ferry, North Carolina, and was admitted to the Hill House General Hospital in Wilmington the next day. On March 5, 1865, he died of disease contracted while a prisoner. His name is listed on the Civil War Monument.

Kelly, Albert, private. Age: 19. Occupation: sailor. Height: 5' 5 3/4". Hair: brown. Comp: light. Eyes: grey.

He was among those enlisted and mustered by Lieutenant George Nelson Macy on July 18, 1861. He was taken prisoner at the battle of Ball's Bluff, Virginia. During his confinement in Richmond's Libby Prison, he contracted typhoid fever. He was eventually paroled at Fort Monroe on January 25, 1862, and returned to Nantucket shortly thereafter.

He returned to the regiment in December 1862, but on April 24, 1863, was discharged for disability, on account of consumption. He returned to Nantucket and on August 28, 1865, died of tuberculosis.

Kelly, Timothy T., private. Age: 39. Occupation: laborer. Height: 5' 11". Hair: light. Comp: light. Eyes: Bbue.

Born in Ireland, Kelly was among those enlisted and mustered by Lieutenant George Nelson Macy on July 18, 1861. In September 1862, he was detailed as an officer's servant and for a time, was assigned to George Nelson Macy. For unspecified reasons, he was imprisoned at Fort Independence in March and April of 1863, but was returned to duty in May.

He is listed as deserting Gettysburg on July 15, 1863, although years later his wife claimed on an application for a pension that he had been killed in action at Gettysburg, and the Bureau of Pensions accepted her assertion and approved the application.

Lowell, Samuel, private. Age: 41. Occupation: carpenter. Height: 6' 1". Hair: light. Comp: light. Eyes: blue.

He was among those enlisted and mustered on July 18, 1861, by Lieutenant George Nelson Macy. One of the oldest men in Company I, he was described by William Francis Bartlett, company captain, as "always so quiet and obliging that he won the respect of every man in the company, by whom he was always addressed as Mr. Lowell."

He was wounded and taken prisoner at Ball's Bluff, then sent to Libby Prison in Richmond. On October 24 he was transferred to Salisbury Prison in North Carolina before being released on May 25, 1862. His health broken by his prison experience, he returned to Nantucket and spent the next six months bedridden. He was discharged for disability on January 26, 1863, for "disease of the spine of six months' duration. Is unable to leave his bed."

He remained in Nantucket after the war. In June of 1867 he was examined by a local physician, who noted that his "back [had been] hurt by a strain opposite Ball's Bluff Va. in Maryland in Oct. 1861 in unloading barrels of beef." The physician approved him for a pension. Other physicians and Lowell himself blamed his imprisonment. Much of his later life was spent on crutches and coping with boils on his legs that the physicians of the day were unable to treat.

His last years were spent in Lewiston, Maine. He died on May 12, 1897.

Macy, George Nelson, first lieutenant. Age: 23. Occupation: clerk. Height: 5'9". Hair: brown. Comp: sandy. Eyes: brown.

Macy was living in Boston when the war broke out and he enlisted for three years on July 10, 1861, mustering on August 8. Immediately afterward, he traveled frequently to Nantucket and Martha's Vineyard to recruit islanders to form the nucleus of Company I.

On October 21, 1861, at the battle of Ball's Bluff, he swam the river searching for boats to help transport his stranded regiment across while the Confederates poured fire into the helpless ranks. On November 11 he was promoted to captain and on December 16 was assigned to Company B. After a brief stint as acting brigade quartermaster, on December 2, 1862, Macy was promoted to acting major and given temporary command of the regiment. He personally led the 20th Massachusetts through the streets of Fredericksburg in the bloody fight of December 11, 1862.

Sergeant (later major) John Summerhayes wrote of Macy's conduct during that battle:

> Too much praise cannot be awarded to Major Macy. . . . [He] was everywhere at once. Where the fire was heaviest and our line growing weak, you would find him encouraging the men to stand firm and do their duty. Shell and ball whistled by him, striking down to the earth the strong and weak, yet he escaped unharmed. He seemed to be shielded while giving his orders as cooly and steadily as on our battalion drills.

Macy was promoted to full major on December 18, 1862.

Early in 1863 he was granted two servants, one of whom was Nantucketer Timothy Kelley. On February 16, 1863, he married Mary Hayden, returning to Nantucket for his honeymoon. As the Nantucket *Weekly Mirror* succinctly expressed the purpose of his visit, "For a time, Mars goes to Hymen."

On April 4 he was promoted to lieutenant colonel. Three months later, on July 3, at the battle of Gettysburg, he was shot by a minié ball in the left hand while facing Pickett's Charge. His hand was amputated as a result, and while prostrate at a Gettysburg field hospital, he was promoted to full colonel on July 5 to replace Paul J. Revere, grandson of the Revolutionary War patriot, who had been killed during the battle.

He returned to Boston and ultimately to Nantucket to convalesce. On March 24, 1864, Macy was assigned recruiting duty in Massachusetts for the 20th Regiment. Shortly afterward, he traveled to Philadelphia to have an artificial hand fitted to his left forearm.

On May 6, 1864, at the battle of the Wilderness, he was shot twice while advancing with his men in a suicidal charge intended to buy time to allow his beleaguered comrades to reorganize in the face of Longstreet's furious assault on Federal positions at the hotly contested intersection of the Orange Plank and Brock roads. Major General Alexander Webb, Macy's brigade commander, described the wounds as a gunshot in ". . . the right leg, by a rifle ball, about half way between the knee and the foot, and [Macy was] also wounded in [the] left leg just below the knee."

Macy returned again to Nantucket to convalesce, but reported for duty to the 20th Massachusetts in Virginia in August. On August 14, 1864, at the battle of Deep Bottom, he was attempting to lead his reluctant men in a charge when his second horse of the day was shot from under him and crushed him as it fell. One contemporary account describes Macy at Deep Bottom, and also reveals something about the psychology of Civil War command:

> Arriving at the front [Macy] was ordered to the command of a brigade, and was directed to charge upon the enemy's works. His horse was soon shot, and he dismounted without injury, and was advised by General Barlow to "go on foot." But the work in hand was of a desperate nature, and the sight of their leader on foot would tend to dispirit the men, who would then infer that he feared to expose himself on horseback. He resolved to go on a horse, and General Barlow then tendered him his own trusty steed, which was accepted. They had proceeded but a short distance when his horse was shot; and maddened by pain he sprang into an apple tree, where he hung suspended by the branches. The Colonel was thrown violently to the ground, and had only time to turn over, when the horse fell upon him, the animal's breast striking his own. The horse turned a complete somerset over the Colonel, who rose, and though severely hurt, pushed on at the head of his men for a few moments, when he fell and was borne senseless from the field.

In the opinion of Private Arthur M. Rivers, who witnessed the fall, Macy's injuries were severe and Rivers told his parents that his colonel was not likely "to get over it." Macy returned to convalesce on Nantucket for the third time during the war, and was carried from the steamboat in a litter. On September 19, 1864, a Nantucket physician described Macy's wound as a "contusion of the chest and abdomen incurred while in the line of his duty by a fall from his horse at Deep Bottom."

By October 1864, he had returned to the front and was assigned to command the 3rd Brigade, 1st Division, II Army Corps. After reorganization that same month, he was appointed to command the 1st Brigade, 1st Division, of the same corps. On February 6, 1865, he was appointed brigadier general to date from August 14, 1864, for "distinguished conduct at the battle of the Wilderness and at Deep Bottom." On March 16, 1865, he was promoted to Provost Marshal of the Army Headquarters, Army of the Potomac.

Major General Joshua Lawrence Chamberlain, in *The Passing of the Armies*, remembers Macy as he passed before the presidential reviewing stand at the Grand Review held in Washington, D. C., on May 23, 1865: "Now rides the provost marshal general, gallant George Macy of the 20th Massachusetts, his right arm [*sic*] symbolized by an empty sleeve pinned across his breast."

After the war, Macy returned to Boston and became an officer with the Suffolk Bank. For his wartime injuries, he was entitled to a pension of $30 per month. On June 22, 1867, he was promoted to brevet major general of volunteers, to date from April 9, 1865, for "gallant and meritorious services during the recent operations resulting in the fall of Richmond, Virginia, and the surrender of the insurgent army under General Robert E. Lee."

He died in a freak accident on February 13, 1875, when his pistol accidentally discharged after he slipped while climbing the front steps to his home in Boston. By Congressional Act, dated March 3, 1903, his wife was awarded his pension, including accruals.

After the death of her second husband, Macy's wife returned to Nantucket and lived in the home she had inherited from her first husband, George Nelson Macy, at 123 Main Street.

Macy is buried in Forest Hills Cemetery in Boston.

Morris, Charles A., private. Age: 34. Occupation: blacksmith. Height: 5' 4". Hair: black. Comp: dark. Eyes: blue.

He enlisted and mustered on August 14, 1862, and joined the regiment at Alexandria on August 29. On December 11, 1862, he was killed in action at the battle of Fredericksburg.

His name is on the Civil War Monument.

Murphey, Franklin Barnard, private. Age: 32. Occupation: mariner. Height: 5' 3". Hair: light. Comp: light. Eyes: blue.

He enlisted and mustered on August 19, 1862. On September 17 he was wounded in the left knee at Antietam. On the march from that battle to Harpers Ferry, he was one of those who fell ill. On November 1, he was admitted to the II Corps Field Hospital at Boliver Heights with diarrhea and was transferred on November 23 to a larger facility in Frederick, Maryland. He was finally returned to duty on March 14, 1863.

But he never fully recovered from his wounded knee. In June 1863 he was admitted to Fairfax General Hospital in Fairfax, Virginia, with "chronic rheumatism." The admitting physician noted: "General Health good but is used up." His knee failed to heal, and on November 6, he was discharged for disability. The army doctor gave as a reason: "Rheumatic. . . left knee joint. [Has] inability to use left leg, contracted since enlistment."

Although the same doctor opined that he was unfit for the Veteran Reserve Corps, Murphey nonetheless enlisted and mustered in Company K, 10th Veteran Reserve Corps, on September 2, 1864. He was promoted to corporal, date unknown, and mustered out on November 14, 1865, expiration of service.

He returned to Nantucket after the war. In 1866, a local physician noted that he had a "bad left knee—from fall in the night in march from Falmouth Va. to Gettysburgh (*sic*)—discharged on that account." He joined the local chapter of the G.A.R. in 1867. By 1883, he was pensioned at $8 per month for "rheumatism at the knee." His chief occupation was as a printer. He was very active in the Nantucket chapter of the G. A. R. and joined during its island revival in 1891. He eventually served as post commander and in other offices.

He died on December 20, 1920, and is buried on the south side of Prospect Hill Cemetery on Nantucket.

Murphey, Josiah F., private. Age: 19. Occupation: grocery store clerk. Height: 5'3 1/2". Hair: light. Comp: fair. Eyes: blue.

He enlisted and mustered on August 12, 1862, and joined the regiment at Alexandria on August 29. On December 11, 1862, at the battle of Fredericksburg, he was shot in the face and hospitalized for four days at the Lacy House, headquarters of Major General Edwin V. Sumner's Right Grand Division and also a field hospital.

He remained four days, then was furloughed to accompany the body of Company I Lieutenant Leander F. Alley, killed at Fredericksburg on December 13. Following a three-month furlough, he rejoined Company I, which was still camped at Falmouth, Virginia. He participated with his regiment in the battle of Chancellorsville. On June 19, 1863, while en route to Gettysburg, Murphey contracted typhoid fever, and on June 23, was admitted to 2nd Division U.S.A. General Hospital (Baptist Church Branch) in Alexandria. He recovered and rejoined his regiment in October 1863.

He was promoted to orderly sergeant in 1864, and was given command of companies C and E briefly before his discharge. He was discharged on August 1, 1864, by reason of expiration of service.

He returned to Nantucket after the war and was engaged in a variety of occupations including butcher, clothing manufacturer, and hardware store owner. In 1866, a local physician found him to be "feeble and dizzy" as a consequence of his wound. The sight in his right eye, impaired from the wound, gradually failed with age. He joined the local G. A. R. during its first island incarnation in 1866. He left the first organization in 1873, shortly before it disbanded. In 1870, he married Avis Nelson Folger. They would have two children.

In 1870, Dr. John B. King of Nantucket examined Murphey and filed with the Pension Bureau the most complete report describing his injury:

> He was struck by a ball . . . on right side of face over malar bone, an inch from outer angle of eye. . . . The right eye is defective in vision & has been so since the wound occurred. It is frequently inflamed, & at all times is weak. The eschar is tender. Pain is severe about it, & shooting from it in wet weather. The neuralgic pains, and the frequent inflammation of the eye incapacitates him for continuous labor.

In 1883 he was receiving a pension of $3 for his Fredericksburg wound. In 1888 physical examination found the wound to be "An

irregular puckering scar two inches in length over right malar promi-
nence extending backward to the ear—Scar is depressable with loss
of boney tissue beneath seat of scar, adherent, dragging and tender."
In 1888 he received a pension of $8 per month. It was raised to
$21.50 in 1913, $27 in 1918, and $38 later that year.

He was a founding member of the reborn G.A.R. chapter on
Nantucket in 1891. During the period between 1891 and 1931, the
general membership reached a high of fifty-two (1893) to three in
1931. In the years between 1891 and 1920, Murphey was post
commander seven times, and held various official positions each year.

Myrick, William H., private. Age: 25. Occupation: shoemaker.
Height: 5' 7". Hair: light. Comp: light. Eyes: blue.

He enlisted and mustered the same day as Josiah F. Murphey on August
12, 1862.

In 1863 a Nantucket physician noted he "received a wound in the
right shoulder from a Gun lock injuring the Scapula," in consequence
of which his "right arm is impaired in strength, and he is unable to
labor at many employments." Myrick described the incident as an
accidental discharge of his shouldered musket while he was carrying
a corpse off the battlefield at Fredericksburg. He was discharged for
disability due to chronic diarrhea on June 5, 1863.

After the war he moved to Brockton, Massachusetts, and found
work in a shoe factory, but was soon forced to quit because of faint-
ing spells, which he attributed to his wartime service. He eventually returned to Nantucket where he died of consumption on November
14, 1877. Dr. John B. King of Nantucket, one of Myrick's attending
physicians during his final illness, refused to submit a bill on account
of Myrick's poverty.

He is buried on the south side of Prospect Hill Cemetery on
Nantucket.

Nicholson, George W., **2nd**, private. Age: 17. Occupation:
sailor/student. Height: 5'5". Hair: dark. Comp: fair. Eyes: blue.

He enlisted and mustered on August 13, 1862, and joined the regiment at Alexandria on August 29. He was discharged for disability on March 3, 1863. His army physician noted: "He suffers from an old sprain of one of his ankles, causing him invariably to give out after two days hard marching. He is besides constitutionally weak. The spring campaign would certainly disable him. He is also light headed at times."

On January 4, 1864, he enlisted in Co. K, Second Massachusetts Cavalry, and was wounded in the right leg at Rockville, Maryland, on July 13, 1864. According to one comrade, Nicholson was "wounded in the leg below the knee, splintering but not materially injuring the bone." He mustered out on June 30, 1865, expiration of service.

He returned to Nantucket after the war and joined the local chapter of the G. A. R. in its first incarnation in 1866.

Orpin, Edward P., private. Age: 22. Occupation: farmer. Height: 5'3". Hair: brown. Comp: light. Eyes: blue.

He was among those enlisted and mustered by Lieutenant George Nelson Macy on July 18, 1861. On December 11, 1862, at the battle of Fredericksburg, he was wounded in the leg.

He reenlisted at Stevensburg, Virginia, for three years on March 19, 1864. As part of the inducement offered to all reenlistees, he received a thirty-day furlough. On May 1, 1864, he is reported to have deserted while on furlough. No further record exists.

Paddock, Thomas Edward, private. Age: 21. Occupation: sailor.

He was among those enlisted and mustered by Lieutenant George Nelson Macy on July 18, 1861. On December 28, 1862, he became sick with an undisclosed illness, for which he was hospitalized until early 1864. On April 6, 1864, he transferred to Co. I, 21st Veteran Reserve Corps. He was discharged August 16, 1864, probably by expiration of service.

Parker, Albert C., private. Age: 16. Occupation: shoemaker. Height: 5'4". Hair: light. Comp: fair. Eyes: blue.

He enlisted and mustered the same day as Josiah F. Murphey, August 12, 1862, and joined the regiment at Alexandria on August 29. On December 11, 1862, he was wounded in the groin and leg at battle of Fredericksburg.

On March 6, 1863, he was discharged for disability on account of his wound, described by the physician: "Gun shot wound through the penis causing stricture of the uretha. . . . Permanent disability."

He died on November 18, 1930, at Chatham, Massachusetts.

Pease, Benjamin P., private. Age: 18. Occupation: sailor. Height: 5'6 1/2". Hair: dark. Comp: dark. Eyes: grey.

He was among those enlisted and mustered by Lieutenant George Nelson Macy on July 18, 1861. At the battle of Ball's Bluff on October 21, 1861, he swam the Potomac and thus avoided being captured or killed by the victorious Confederates. Years later, he recalled his experiences at that battle:

> Sergt. Riddell was the first wounded man I ever saw and the sight of blood made me feel faint. I soon got used to it, however. We fought till nearly dark when we were told to every man look out for himself. We were bunched in an open space on the top of the bluff and the woods which hemmed us in on three sides seemed to be fairly alive with rebs who made fearful havoc among our boys. When the order came to retreat we scrambled down that bluff in a hurry. At the foot of the bluff I fell in with my cousin George G. Worth, who said, "if they drive us too hard, you and I are good for the river." I never saw him afterward. He was shot while swimming across and drowned. His body was subsequently recovered. The last man I saw on shore was Samuel Lowell. He couldn't swim and was feeling dreadfully because he knew that he would either be shot or taken prisoner. He was subsequently captured and confined in rebel prisons until exchanged.
>
> Finding I must swim for it I threw my rifle and cartridge box into the river, stripped off my clothes and plunged in, and though the rebs were picking off our men at a fearful rate, I was fortunate to get across unharmed. I arrived at the island nearly naked, followed a towpath to Edward's Ferry and staid [sic] there all night.

Pease was promoted to corporal by the Peninsula Campaign of June 1862. He and Sergeant Holmes were referred to by one comrade as "two of the neatest men among us—always on hand when wanted." At the battle of Fredericksburg on December 13, 1862, he was one of the four men who risked enemy fire to retrieve the body of Lieutenant Leander F. Alley.

Pease was promoted to sergeant after Fredericksburg "for bravery." On July 3, 1863, at the battle of Gettysburg, he was shot through the wrist while defending against Pickett's Charge.

He returned to Nantucket in February, 1864, for recruiting duty. Upon his return, he reenlisted as first sergeant on March 3 and received a $325 reenlistment bonus. He was promoted to second lieutenant on April 29. Several days later, at the battle of the Wilderness, he was shot in the right chest, the bullet slowed by a wad of papers in his breast pocket that included his officer's commission signed by Massachusetts Governor John A. Andrew. On the back of this document, which bears a .58-inch hole, Pease wrote:

A musket ball passed through this commission and my discharge paper and into my right side breaking a rib. The papers were in my breast pocket at the battle of the Wilderness May 6, 1864. Was captured at Welden R.R.[sic] Aug. 25, '64. Was in prison 6 months. Libby, Salisbury, Danville.

These papers are in the archives of the Nantucket Historical Association.

Following his capture at the battle of Reams Station on August 25, 1864, he was imprisoned at Libby Prison in Richmond and transferred to Salisbury Prison on October 27. He was paroled at Richmond on February 22, 1865, and returned to Nantucket on March 11. He resigned his commission on June 22 citing "Important Family Affairs and Sickness in the Family." He mustered out as captain of Co. A, 20th Massachusetts Volunteer Infantry, rank dating from June 1, 1865.

He returned to Nantucket after the war and worked as a laborer. He was pensioned at $9 per month for his wrist wound and died of heart disease on July 27, 1904. He is buried in the New North Cemetery on Nantucket.

Perkins, Charles H., private. Age: 18. Occupation: fisherman. Height: 5' 6". Hair: brown. Comp: light. Eyes: grey.

He enlisted and mustered on February 29, 1864, and was discharged as a rejected recruit on April 25, 1864. There is no further record.

Pratt, George C., private. Age: 21. Occupation: shoemaker. Height: 5' 9". Hair: black. Comp: dark. Eyes: grey.

He was among those enlisted and mustered by Lieutenant George Nelson Macy on July 18, 1861.

He was wounded in the head and right hip at battle of Ball's Bluff on October 21, 1861. Years later, he provided this account of his experience:

> About midnight we crossed to the Virginia shore in two boats, (a skiff and pontoon boat), by which our entire force, numbering about 1800, was ferried across by daylight. We ascended the bluff by means of a narrow path, and a skirmish line was sent out to ascertain the whereabouts of the enemy. . . . About 4 o'clock I was knocked down by a bullet wound in the hip. As I got up another bullet struck me in the head. [Comrade Benjamin Whitford testified after the war that "I was looking at (Pratt) when wounded the second time—saw his cap knocked from his head and the blood flow over his face."] Two men were detailed to carry me to camp. I soon fainted from loss of blood and when I came to, found myself lying in the hold of a canal boat with a lot of other wounded men at Edward's Ferry. I managed to crawl on deck and learned it was noon of the 24th, also that the boat I was brought over in was the last to cross the river, it having been sunk on the next trip, and after that all who escaped had to swim.
>
> I was taken on an ambulance carriage, being obliged to ride outside in the rain, to Camp Benton, and placed in the hospital where my wounds were dressed. When I was sufficiently recovered I was granted a month's furlough and came back to Nantucket.

At the battle of Fredericksburg Pratt counted 16 bullet holes in his uniform, although he was miraculously unscathed. On September 23, 1863, he transferred to Co. C, 6th Veteran Reserve Corps for malaria and "palpatations of the heart," and was promoted to corporal, date unknown. He was discharged July 19, 1864, for expiration of service.

He attempted to relocate to Brockton, Massachusetts, after the war to pursue shoemaking, but in spite of several attempts his health forced him to leave his craft. Around 1875 he moved to New Bedford and became a partner in a grocery store. By 1878 his mental state, impaired by his head wound, forced him to abandon his trade.

In 1867, a local physician had described the head injury: "A minnie [sic] ball struck the left Parietal near the top of the head fracturing and causing the loss of a portion of the skull bone. Sudden movement causes dizziness [and Pratt cannot] stoop without danger of falling—Disability three fourths." His hip wound was caused by a bullet entering his right buttock and traveling some eight inches to touch the femur, from which it was removed. The mental effects of his head wound followed him for life, and included incapacitating headaches, vertigo, seizures, and nausea. He was pensioned at $8 per month for a "wound in head."

On January 6, 1914, Pratt died at the age of 73 from "embolism of the coronary artery." He is buried on the south side of Prospect Hill Cemetery on Nantucket.

Randall, Edward W., private/drummer. Age: 18. Occupation: unknown. Height: 5' 3 1/2". Hair: light. Comp: light. Eyes: blue.

He enlisted on July 19, 1862, and joined the regiment at Harrison's Landing on August 4. He reenlisted on February 17, 1864, at Stevensburg, Virginia, and was promoted to corporal in May or June, 1864.

At the Battle of Reams Station on August 25, 1864, he was taken prisoner, and on August 27 was sent to Libby Prison in Richmond. On October 9, he was transferred to Salisbury prison in North Carolina. In February, 1865, he was apparently returned to Libby where he died of disease in the prison hospital on March 2, 1865.

His name is on the Civil War Monument.

Raymond, Charles H., private. Age: 23. Occupation: caulker. Height: 5' 8 1/2". Hair: dark. Comp: sallow. Eyes: blue.

He enlisted and mustered on July 19, 1862, and joined the regiment at Harrison's Landing on August 4. He was wounded at the battle of Antietam on September 17, 1862. A comrade reported:

. . . Private Charles Raymond was shot through the thigh. I saw him fall out of the ranks, and thought he was going to run, so I shoved him back, rebuking him for so doing, as he had heard Lieut. Alley's positive orders for the file closers to make every man stand—even to use the bayonet. He stepped back in the ranks, and as he did not appear at all unnerved, I left him to go elsewhere. As I turned, one of the boys called to me saying that Raymond was wounded. I informed the Lieutenant, who immediately ordered him to the rear; but go he would not, sitting down behind the rank, exposed the same as all the others, he remained looking coolly on.

On July 2, 1863, at the battle of Gettysburg, Raymond deserted "his colors in the face of the enemy." He was court-martialed, found guilty, and sentenced to the dreaded Union prison at Dry Tortugas for the unexpired term of his service and the forfeit of $10 of his $13 monthly pay. He never went farther south than the Old Capitol Prison in Washington, D.C. His sentence was remitted and he was released in November 1863, "upon condition that he shall make good the time lost by desertion."

On February 11, 1864, Raymond was detailed as a hospital steward, but he returned to the ranks for the spring campaign of 1864. Sometime during the Wilderness Campaign he was taken prisoner by the Confederates.

On June 12, 1864, he died while confined at the notorious Confederate prison at Andersonville, Georgia. The cause of death was "variola," a fatally acute viral form of smallpox.

Raymond's name is on the Civil War Monument.

Rivers, Alonzo M., private. Age: 18. Occupation: student. Height: 5' 9". Hair: light brown. Comp: fair. Eyes: blue.

He enlisted and mustered on July 19, 1862, and joined the regiment at Harrison's Landing, Virginia, on August 4. Beginning in September 1862, he was marked absent due to illness, and on January 21, 1863, he was discharged for disability. The army physician found Rivers incapable of performing the duties of a soldier because of "great functional disturbance of the action of the heart, chronic diarrhea, youth & general debility contracted in the service."

Rivers, Arthur M., private. Age: claimed 17, but was in fact 15. Occupation: farmer. Height: 5' 6". Hair: dark. Comp: fair. Eyes: black.

He enlisted on August 13, 1862 and mustered on August 15 before joining the regiment at Alexandria on August 29. He was among those falling ill after the march from Antietam to Harpers Ferry, and was hospitalized from November 1862, until March 1863.

On July 3, 1863, at the battle of Gettysburg, he was shot through the chest while defending against Pickett's Charge. His wound was described by the Nantucket *Weekly Mirror*: "It entered above his left hip, splintering the bone, and passed through his body, breaking the lower rib on the right side, and lodging in the flesh over the rib." In spite of the serious nature of the wound, the *Mirror* stated as of August 29 that "he has nearly recovered from its effects, and is again nearly ready to go 'marching along.'" But Private Rivers was to remain in hospital for another five months.

Following his return to duty, he contracted a debilitating facial rash which his doctors attributed to contact with some poisonous plant while on picket. He returned to hospital again, and was not released until May 1864.

In spite of doubts, he reenlisted February 15, 1864, to the credit of Reading, Massachusetts, and received a $325 bonus. He was taken prisoner by victorious Confederates at the battle of Reams Station on August 25, 1864.

Five letters written by Private Rivers survive and deserve reproducing here for the information they contain about the life and times of their author as well as several of his Nantucket comrades from Company I. The letters have been edited only to the extent of adding periods to better demarcate sentences.

Patterson Park Hosp Bal
Jan 10. 1864

Dear Mother

I now sit down to write you a few lines to inform you that I am well hoping this will find you the same. we have had verry cold and stormy weather for quite a time past. we have had a hard snow storm & the folks improved it. their was nice sleighing for one day & then it froze & it was splendid. it has been cold weather every where to see by the papers + a number have froze to death in Ohio mostly rebel prisoners who were confined there. it is a grate pity that the whole of them did not freeze. tell frank to write & I will write to him. the small pox has got into the hospital though when any one gets it they are carried to the marine hospital down by fort McHenry. I have been vaccinated in three places & it took real nice on both of my arms so I do not think that I shall get it. their is a large pond back of the hospital where we can go & skate. you said in your last letter that frank had got a nother furlough. does his mother fret as much as ever about him[?] it seem to mee that he gets a furlough quite often for one that that had always been in the hospital. I wish that I could get one so easy though. I guess that he is not of any account & they send him of[f] to get clear of him. he says that he has not got any pay yet. I know that he has for the invalid corpse has all been paid here last week & it seem[ed] strange why he does not get it when every one else does. I guess that he fools his mother & spends his all himself which I would not do. we are to be paid of[f] this week for we have signed the pay rolls yesterday. if I get paid I will send home enough for the [illegible]. I did not get any this last week. did you send it[?] they are enlisting quite smart here. there was two regiments went through here last night for home. they were the 4 new jersey & a western regiment who had reenlisted for the war. I had a letter from Ned Randall to day. he says that the boy[s] are not going to enlist again. their was only four who reenlisted out of the whole regiment. their was one nantucket boy that was Freeman Cottle. he is color bearer. Macy tried to get the boys to enlist again but they wouldn't se[e] it. we had a nother hard snow storm last night. I went to the theatre with the doctor & had a nice time. they played the french [illegible]. I am going again this week if we get paid of[f]. I began this letter two days ago. I thought I would write a good long one to night is saturday. I have just got through playing cards with the doctor so I thought that I would write a little. we have had it quite pleasant today. mother will you send me that bosom[?] shirt that I left at home. you must not think strange of me for sending for it. while one is two good for a under shirt & that white one is coming all to pieces. I go out a good deal at night & I want something nice. you must not think strange of me for I am a queer chap anyway though I suppose that you know it by this time. I guess that I visit again very soon. has alonzo got his papers yet[?] I have not herd from him since I wrote last. I wish I had the chances to get along that he has had. the shirt you can put in the express for it is colder than I thought it was. it will not cost much to send it. send me some stamps when you write again. the trains have been delayed here on account of the snow so you must not think strange if you do not get my letter as soon as usual. I received a letter from Alonzo & I was disappointed because I did not hear from you. if you want my picture enough to send the money I will have them taken. I had a nice present from one of my friends. it was watch worth about 20 dollars. it is a splendid one. write soon. from your son

Arthur M. Rivers

The second letter was written from Falmouth, Virginia, after the battle of Chancellorsville, in May 1863:

> Camp near falmouth
> Virg May 26 63

Dear parents I now take my pen in hand to write you a few lines & to inform you that I [am] well hoping that this will find you the same. I received your welcome letter yesterday just as we were goying out on drill & was verry glad to hear from you for that is the first letter that I have received since I have crosed the river. you say that you sent me a letter with a dollar bill in it & three papers. I received the papers but not [the] letter. now mother do not send me any more money for we have been paid of[f]. I have not been paid of[f] all that they owe me. I shall send home about 60 dollars this pay day & about

20 dollars every letter now. if you get this one with 20 dollars send me word if you get it. I think that we shall be in the city of fredericksburg before long. old joe hooker has got about 120 thousand men here & about 50 thousand on the peninsula. that 50 thousand are trying to get between lee & richmond & then for us to attack them here but lee has found it out & is evacuating those heghts of frederickburg. we can see them moveing off while I am writing. they are cutting all of their grass to carry with them but I must stop for I have to work now.

from

Arthur H. Rivers

enclosed you will find 20 dollars

The third letter was written shortly before the army moved out to meet Lee's invasion of Pennsylvania.

Camp near Falmouth

Virg June 9 / 63

Dear parents I now take my pencil in hand to write you a few lines to inform you that I am well hoping that this will find you the same. I received your letters [and] every thing that you have sent. if you do not get my letter as soon as you ought to you must not think anything about it for we are fighting now. we are across the river now in our entrenchments which we took from the rebels two day ago. we have got them in a tite place. the army on the peninsula is in them now so that they cannot retreat to richmond. so I must stop for this time. I shall send 20 dollars this time so good by.

from your son

A M Rivers

send me about 12 stamps

if you want to use this money use it. do not put in the bank
now remember

The fourth letter was written a week before Private Rivers was taken prisoner by the Confederates at the battle of Reams Station.

Camp of the 20 Mass near
Deep Bottom-Vir on pickett-Aug 18/64

Dear Parents

I thought I would write to inform you that I am well hoping you are the same. I arrived at my Regiment the first of this month. we are now on some kind of an Expedition what for I do not know. we had a fight last sunday & Col Macy led us on a charge. he had two horses shot from under him. the last fell on him & hurt him very badly. I do not think he will get over it. they have sent him home. he was only with us one day. we have but a verry small Regiment. we have lost 41 men and officers in this concern. Major Pattern was wound[ed] & lost his leg. it is pretty warm work on picket. if you show yourself at all the rebels fire at you. Birney['s] Corp the 10 has lost between 3 & 4 thousand [illegible] somewhere in the neighborhood of Malvern Hill. how long we have to stay here I do not know. we had an awful hard cannonading on our right last night. Ned Randall is here all right. have you heard from alonzo lately[?] I have not heard from him since I left home. did you get that picture of Randall & myself that I sent by Clay Farnum[?] their is but 4 Nantucket boys in Com[pany]. I [k]now we have 117 men belonging to it & their is three regiments consolidated to gether the 15 & 19 & [illegible] with us. Lieut Pease commands the company. answer this & direct too

> A.M. Rivers
>
> Comp I 20 Mass VV
> Washington, D.C.

their is some talk of our getting paid up to the last of July. they owe me $12. send me the American Union & some stamps when you write again"

The next letter was written four days after his capture and is post-marked "Old Point Comfort, Va," a frequent exchange place between Union and Confederate armies.

Richmond Aug 29 64

Dear Parents

I now write to inform you that I am well. I was captured at Reams Station on the Weldon Rail Road. our whole Regiment was captured on the 25 of Aug. Their is Ned Randall John Barnard Sam Crocker Lieut Pease of Nantu-

I send this by flag of truce [illegible]

I am in Libby Prison. answer this direct to
A.M. Rivers Libby Prison Richmond Va or elsewhere"

Private Rivers was later transferred to the Confederate POW camp at Salisbury, North Carolina. On December 22, 1864, still a prisoner of war, he died from diarrhea, although the the Nantucket *Weekly Mirror* believed otherwise, as it stated in his obituary:

Private Rivers was severely wounded at the battle of Gettysburg, and for a long time his life was despaired of. On regaining his strength he immediately joined his command, and was taken prisoner at Reams' Station in August. The sufferings and privations he endured while a prisoner, caused his wound to break out afresh, and he died on December 21st. He was perfectly resigned to his fate, and stated that if he could only breathe, his last under the stars and stripes he should be happy, but felt it hard to die under the secession flag. Thus at the early age of only seventeen years died one of the purest patriots and bravest soldiers that ever gave his life for his country, and one of whose memory his surviving and sorrowing parents may well feel proud.

His body was returned to Nantucket and is buried in Prospect Hill Cemetery. His name is on the Civil War Monument.

Russell, Thomas J., private. Age: 20. Occupation: hostler. Height: 5'11". Hair: light. Comp: fair. Eyes: blue.

He enlisted and mustered on August 14, 1862. On December 11, 1862, he helped row one of the boats across the Rappahannock River in the assault on Fredericksburg. Later, a minié ball passed through his left thigh as he advanced through the streets of the town.

On July 1, 1863, he transferred to Company A, 14th Veteran Reserve Corps, and was discharged on July 24, 1864, by reason of expiration of service. Six weeks later he enlisted in Company M of the 2nd Massachusetts Heavy Artillery to the credit of the town of Sandsfield, Massachusetts. On December 16 he transferred to Company F of the 17th Massachusetts Volunteer Infantry and was discharged on June 30, 1865, probably by reason of expiration of service.

He moved to New Hampshire after the war and worked in a sawmill, eventually moving to the New Hampshire Soldiers' Home in Tilton. He died there on July 2, 1923, at the age of 81.

Ryder, George F., private. Age: 24. Occupation: shoemaker. Height: 5' 10 3/4". Hair: dark. Comp: dark. Eyes: grey.

Although born in Wareham, Ryder was employed in a candle factory on Nantucket when war broke out. On July 26, 1861, he enlisted and mustered although to the credit of Duxbury, Massachusetts, where he had been working as a shoemaker.

He claimed that the exertion of swimming the Potomac during the panic following the disaster at Ball's Bluff caused a prolapsed rectum. He was dicharged for disability on March 27, 1862 due to "ulceration of the rectum."

He returned to Duxbury and served as a recruiter for the town. On September 22, 1862, he enlisted in Company I, 4th Massachusetts

Volunteer Militia. According to one account, the Duxbury quota was one short when Ryder volunteered to fill it. Assigned to light duty, Ryder was apparently serving as a sharpshooter when a near miss from a shell blinded him. He was to suffer permanently impaired vision although from a different cause. Years later, Ryder remembered:

> [In June 1863] During the seige at Port Hudson one night after being relieved from duty as Corporal of the guard, I sat down facing the enemy's works and fell asleep, and was suddenly awakened by some means just as a shell exploded in the air in front of and very near to me, the light of which blinded me for a few moments and after that my eyes pained me some until I was taken sick with what we called ground scurvy, but I never supposed this explosion had much to do with the affection of my eyes, as the Doctor told me it was the scurvy which worked mostly about the upper part of my person and head which affected my eyes.

Dr. Joseph F. Gould, assistant surgeon of the 4th Massachusetts, later described Ryder's ailment as "iritis"—a severe inflammation of the eyes. He was discharged September 23, 1863, expiration of service.

After the war, Ryder moved to South Duxbury. Disabled by his injuries, he became a "peddlar selling goods on the road." He died on April 29, 1918, of arteriosclerosis.

Sanford, George H., private. Age: 30. Occupation: farmer. Height: 5' 10". Hair: dark. Comp: dark. Eyes: blue.

He enlisted and mustered on July 26, 1862. On September 17, at the Battle of Antietam, Sanford injured his knee while attempting to mount a stone wall. After the war, he gave this account of his injury and its aftermath:

> When We Went in the Battle of Aunteen We Was ordered From the center to go to the Right to suport a Battery and in going to the right by going over a pile of stones i sprained my Knee but i didint feel it Then until the next day. it Pained and i sat at a camp Fire and Was rubbing my knee. And George Backus came along And asked me What Was the Mater and i told him that i Had sprained my knee and Leutenant Macy and a Leutenant that i didint know. The Leutenant that Was With Leutenant Macy asked Who is that young man that [was] there by the fire and he said that Was one of our new Recrutes that had just come Out. When we went on a march I had to fall out because i Could not keep up With the Regiment. We Went to balliver height. We stopped two Weaks. We Was ordered to go on a march Again and i Went as far [as] Warinton junction. then i Was sent to Washington and Went to Capital hil horspital. . . .

On February 23, 1863, Sanford was discharged for disability at Convalescent Camp in Washington, D.C., by reason of "functional disease of heart existing three months contacted in service." He returned to Nantucket, and on August 13, 1864, with the expectation that he would be spared marching, Sanford reenlisted in Company K, 12th Veteran Reserve Corps. Years later, he recalled the experience and revealed something of an attitude about Civil War medicine:

> And then i Went to Boston and enlisted under major Clark and He told me that they Was not Given anny bounty but if they Gave anny i should be intitled To it. i Was sent to camp day 22 Miles from boston. . . . They sent us to Washington to Do hospital duty and When [I] got There [I] went on duty. there i Was Detached to fetch Water. While i was fetching the Water my knee gave out. then some of [the] Doctors Wanted me to go in the hospital and have my knee Worked upon and doctor Craft advised me not to for if [I] Did i should lose my leg. I thought that a Whole leg Was Better than a half one. . . .

The army offered Sanford a discharge for disability, but he declined: "I told [the doctor] that i didint want For i had nowhere to go then For i had no home so i stayed enlisted until they broke up. . . ." While with the Veteran Reserve Corps, Sanford also served as a guard at the Old Capitol Prison in Washington. He was discharged November 14, 1865, by expiration of service.

He returned to Nantucket after the war, and worked as a "laborer." In 1866, a local physician noted during an examination of his left knee that he had a "loose tendon or ligament on external aspect. Gives out entirely so often as to make total inability to earn a living by labor." He was awarded a pension of $8 per month.

In 1891, he joined the Nantucket chapter of the G. A. R. during its island revival. He died at the age of 67 on February 25, 1900, of typhoid fever and pneumonia, and is buried at South Cemetery on Nantucket.

Snow, George E., private. Age: 21. Occupation: farmer. Height: 5'9". Hair: dark. Comp: dark. Eyes: grey.

He enlisted and mustered on July 26, 1862, and joined the regiment on September 4 at Rockville, Maryland. He was killed in action at the battle of Fredericksburg on December 11, 1862.

His name is on the Civil War Monument.

Stackpole, Albert, private. Age: 18. Occupation: farmer.

He was among those enlisted and mustered by Lieutenant George Nelson Macy on July 18, 1861. He was shot by a minié ball in the right groin at the battle of Ball's Bluff on October 21, 1861. Then company captain William Francis Bartlett wrote of Stackpole: "He bore his sufferings with courage and patience. We buried him as a soldier on Sunday last, Oct. 27th. A small inscription marks his grave, near the main road leading to the Ferry."

His name is on the Civil War Monument.

Starbuck, George B., private. Age: 22. Occupation: farmer. Height: 6'. Hair: black. Comp: dark. Eyes: hazel.

He enlisted and mustered on August 19, 1862. On May 12, 1864, he was wounded by a gunshot in the right hand at the battle of Spotsylvania, and on May 20 was admitted to Lincoln General Hospital in Washington, D. C. He was treated for the wound and for "intermittent fevers." On July 11, he was transferred to Boston, and was discharged for wounds on August 1, 1864.

Starbuck is buried on the north side of Prospect Hill Cemetery on Nantucket.

Summerhayes, John W., private. Age: 25. Occupation: mechanic. Height: 5'5". Hair: light brown. Comp: light. Eyes: blue.

One of the organizers of the Island Guard, the militia unit formed on Nantucket immediately after Fort Sumter, Summerhayes enlisted and mustered on September 9, 1861, and was sent to Camp Cameron for training.

On October 21, 1861, at the battle of Ball's Bluff, he was shot in the foot. On November 1 he was promoted to corporal, and then detached for recruiting duty for several months between late 1861 and early 1862.

Summerhayes received two undisclosed wounds during the 1862 Peninsula Campaign, once "slightly" at Allen's Farm on June 29 and again at Savage Station on July 2. It was on the Peninsula that he personally accepted the surrender of Confederate General James Johnston Pettigrew. Summerhayes's commanding officer presented him with General Pettigrew's pistols, and he sent them to Nantucket, where his father placed them on exhibition in the "Ambrotype Salon" in the family photography shop on Main Street. Summerhayes wrote home about the episode:

> Lieutenant Abbott ordered me into the woods, with a file of men, to bring out all the wounded, and rebels, that could be found. As I started, seven came out, belonging to the Hampton Legion, S.C., the finest brigade in the rebel service. After coming in with them, I advanced into the woods, and hearing a groaning, walked up and there found Lieut. Col. Bull, of the 34th Georgia. I took his sword and revolver, and sent him in. After taking several more, I fell in with one, whom I knew, although his side arms were gone, was of some high rank, and so he proved to be. Although he would not give me any answers, the Colonel was more fortunate, for he found out that it was Brigadier General Pettigrew, of the State of South Carolina.

Summerhayes was promoted to sergeant major on January 1, 1863. and on April 9 was promoted to second lieutenant and assigned to Company C. By the battle of Gettysburg, he had been transferred to Company G.

On July 3, 1863, after Pickett's Charge, he captured the sword of Confederate General Richard Brook Garnett, a principal leader of the ill-fated assault. He sent the sword to Nantucket. On September 9, he was promoted to first lieutenant, and on October 10, to captain.

In May 1864, at the battle of the Wilderness, he was wounded a fourth time when he was shot through the wrist. Shortly afterward he was assigned to 2nd Division staff, II Corps, and on June 29 he was appointed division inspector. Citing "urgent personal reasons" (during the last year of the war, his family had been plagued by deaths), he resigned his commission and was honorably discharged on June 5, 1865. He was later breveted major, United States Volunteers, to date April 9, 1865, for "Meritorious service in the recent campaign terminating with the surrender of the insurgent army under General Robert E. Lee."

After two years of civilian life, Summerhayes returned to the regular army and was appointed second lieutenant in the 33rd United States Infantry. In 1874, he married Martha Dunham of Nantucket. Later, she would record her experiences as an army wife in the unsettled Arizona Territory in her memoirs, *Vanishing Arizona*— a classic of western literature,

Summerhayes remained a career soldier through the Spanish–American War, achieving the rank of lieutenant colonel and becoming the paymaster for the army. Following a severe bout of depression and a "nervous breakdown," he retired from the army in 1900. Like so many of his Civil War comrades, he was plagued with a lifetime of chronic diarrhea and bowel complaints following his Civil War service.

He suffered from angina pectoris, and died March 8, 1911, at the age of 76. He is buried in Arlington National Cemetery.

Swain, Charles F., private. Age: 23. Occupation: farmer. Height: 5' 6". Hair: light. Comp: light. Eyes: blue.

He enlisted and mustered on August 19, 1862. He was wounded at the battle of Fredericksburg on December 11 by a gunshot wound in the left shoulder and cheek, described as "Buck shot head-minnie ball through shoulders." On July 1, 1863, he transferred to Company A, 9th Veteran Reserve Corps. He was discharged August 23, 1864, expiration of service. He reenlisted in Company A of the 1st Maine Sharpshooters on October 27, 1864. He was discharged July 1, 1865.

Swain returned to Nantucket after the war. In 1866 a physician found him to be suffering from a "weakness of arm and head & eyes." In 1891, he joined the Nantucket chapter of the G. A. R. during its island revival. He died on October 26, 1909, and is buried on Nantucket.

Swain, William C., private. Age: 18. Occupation: farmer. Height: 5'9". Hair: light. Comp: fair. Eyes: blue.

He enlisted and mustered on August 21, 1862, and joined the regiment at Alexandria on August 29. He was reportedly wounded "slightly," date and location undisclosed. He was discharged for disability on January 21, 1863, but not for wounds. Dr. B. F. Taft, assistant surgeon of the regiment, gave the reasons: "Incapacity, he being slow to comprehend anything that is told him, and his memory is so poor that he forgets, in a short time, what has been said to him; he is unable to go through the drill from these causes." Taft also noted that "His disability occurred before his enlistment so that he has never been fit for a single day's duty." There is no further record.

Swain, Jacob G., private. Age: 18. Occupation: farmer. Height: 5'6". Hair: light. Comp: fair. Eyes: blue.

He enlisted and mustered on August 14, 1862, and joined the regiment at Alexandria on August 29. On December 11, his left knee was fractured by a minié ball at the battle of Fredericksburg. On December 13, his leg was amputated from the lower third of the thigh. He was transferred to Douglas Hospital in Washington, D.C., where, on February 13, 1863, he wrote his mother and sisters that "My health is good, & my wound is healing slowly, but well, & fast as can be expected." However, the prospects for returning home were not good:

As to your looking or expecting me home every day you will look in vain for awhile for I shall not be able to come if I could get a Furlough under three or four weeks, & they have issued an order, that no Amputation cases ever have a Furlough, but will have to remain until able to be discharged. So you can see that the prospect is fair for me to stay sometime. Now do not think & worry about me so that you cannot have any peace of mind, for I am with those that feels some interest in my wellfare, & if you were here, you would think that I had some good times. seeing the rest, if I cannot join in their sports, there are some ladies in the City, that come & see me; & I get an occasionall piece of Pie, & cake, from their hands. I can assure you that I shall know how to appreciate Home, & its Comforts, if I am favored to return. I have not taken any Medicine since I have been here, so that you can see that I am not sick; I can eat anything in the shape of food; or fruit; & it does not hurt me.

By June, Swain had been transferred to the General Hospital at 65th and Vine Streets in Philadelphia. He wrote to his two sisters on June 14:

We all went to the City the other day to a kind of a party had a nice time. I am to get my leg here (probably a reference to his being fitted with an artificial leg). . . . They are having a meeting here this afternoon and I can here them preach while writing.

On October 8, Swain's leg was reamputated higher up the thigh in an attempt to stem an infection that had set in at the original amputation site. On October 20 he died from "excessive burrowing of pus and disintegration of the stump," which followed the reamputation.

On October 31, 1863, the Nantucket *Weekly Mirror* published his obituary with the heading "Another Volunteer Gone." It stated, in part:

[Swain] was an enterprising young man, about twenty years of age [who] was spoken of by the members of that company in high terms as a young man of promise. At the first battle of Fredericksburg, he was so badly injured as to require the amputation of the left leg, and since that time, in consequence of diseased bone, has had to undergo the third operation. Until within a few days of his death he was expecting to recover, and would cheerfully say he should yet do good service for his country, with a wooden limb. He was a good son and kind brother, and his early death is very much lamented.

> He the young and strong that cherished,
> Noble longings for the strife,
> By the road-side fell and perished,
> With the weary march of life.

Swain was buried in Glenwood Cemetery in Philadelphia. His name is on the Civil War Monument.

Swain, William H., private. Age: 20. Occupation: farmer. Height: 5' 6". Hair: red. Comp: light. Eyes: hazel.

He enlisted and mustered on August 19, 1862. On December 11, 1862, he was killed in action at the battle of Fredericksburg. His body was returned to Nantucket and is buried on the south side of Prospect Hill Cemetery.

His name is on the Civil War Monument.

Swain, William K., private. Age: 18. Occupation: farmer. Height: 5'6". Hair: brown. Comp: dark. Eyes: blue.

He enlisted and mustered the same day as Josiah F. Murphey, on August 12, 1862. Among those who fell ill after the march from Antietam to Harpers Ferry, he died of typhoid fever at Boliver Heights, Virginia, on October 16, 1862, The Nantucket *Mirror* commented on his death: "He was beloved by all who knew him."

His name is on the Civil War Monument.

Swan, William F., private. Age: 44. Occupation: sailor. Height: 5'6". Hair: light. Comp: fair. Eyes: blue. Born in Essex, England.

He enlisted and mustered on August 14, 1862. Sometime after the battle of Gettysburg, he became ill and was dropped from the rolls shortly thereafter. On January 16, 1864, Swan was discharged for disability, and there is some evidence that his true age was 54. The army physician gave as his reasons for discharging him: "Obesity and varicose veins contracted since enlistment—Degree of disability two thirds—also old age . . . unfit for Invalid Corps."

Waterman, Nelson, private. Age: 19. Occupation: shoemaker. Height: 5'4". Hair: brown. Comp: light. Eyes: blue.

He enlisted and mustered the same day as Josiah F. Murphey on August 12, 1862. He was among those who fell ill on the march from Antietam to Harpers Ferry. On October 18, 1862, he was discharged for disability from the Finley General Hospital in Washington, D. C. with lung disease.

He returned to Nantucket after the war. In 1866, a local physician found that while he still suffered from "rheumatism & chronic diarrhea," he seemed "pretty well now," and thus did not qualify for a pension that year. He joined the local chapter of the G. A. R. during its first island incarnation.

He is buried on the north side of Prospect Hill Cemetery on Nantucket.

Whitford, Benjamin H., corporal. Age: 33. Occupation: auctioneer. Height: 5'8 1/2". Hair: light. Comp: light. Eyes: blue.

A fervent speaker for the Union cause at patriotic meetings on Nantucket, Whitford enlisted and mustered on July 31, 1861. At the battle of Ball's Bluff he swam the Potomac to avoid capture. He fell ill afterward and for the rest of his life attributed his chronic rheumatism to exposure in the cold waters of the Potomac.

Eight months later, he participated in the siege of Yorktown. He was discharged on September 10, 1862, to enlist as hospital steward in the regular army, receiving his appointment on September 16. He was discharged on April 18, 1866, with his commanding officer noting that his character was "excellent."

He returned to Nantucket after the war, and in 1867 joined the local chapter of the G. A. R. during its first island incarnation. He died from "chronic rheumatism" on August 12, 1884, in Pennsylvania.

Wilcomb, James A., private. Age: 22. Occupation: seaman. Height: 5' 9". Hair: brown. Comp: dark. Eyes: dark.

Before joining the regiment, he served in the U. S. Navy from August 1861 until April 1862. He was wounded in action on board the USS *Cairo* during the capture of Fort Donelson in February 1862, when a splinter loosened by an explosion pierced his left arm. He was discharged in April as a result of the injury.

Wilcomb enlisted and mustered in the 20th Massachusetts on August 5, 1862. During the march from Antietam to Harpers Ferry he suffered a hernia, for which he was hospitalized. He returned to the ranks but was hospitalized periodically for "scorbutic diarrhea" and "dyspepsia." He was discharged for disability on February 16, 1863 for "valvular disease of the heart contracted in service—Disability 3/4."

He returned to Nantucket after the war and worked as a fisherman. In 1867, two Nantucket physicians testified that Wilcomb was three-quarters disabled "chiefly on account of [a] lame & weak back consequent upon the injury received on board the Gun-boat. . . . He now suffers with lame and weak back & with Fever & Ague, & with difficulty about passing water."

He died on June 24, 1881, at the age of forty, from consumption, and is buried on the south side of Prospect Hill Cemetery on Nantucket.

Wilcomb, William H., private. Age: 19. Occupation: sailor.

He mustered sometime after August 18, 1862, the date of his marriage to sixteen-year-old Mary A. Wilcomb. On December 11, 1862, he was killed in action at the battle of Fredericksburg. Captain Arthur R. Curtis of Company I stated: "He was shot in the stomach . . . & died almost instantly from the effects of his wound. He was a good soldier." In 1863 his widow was awarded a pension of $8 a month.

His name is on the Civil War Monument.

Winslow, William H., private. Age: 39. Occupation: mariner. Height: 5'5". Hair: light. Comp: light. Eyes: blue.

A veteran of many whaling voyages, he first shipped out when he was ten years old. He enlisted and mustered the same day as Josiah F. Murphey, on August 12, 1862, and joined the regiment at Alexandria on August 29. On December 11, 1862, he was killed in action at the battle of Fredericksburg.

His obituary described him as:

. . . low spoken, and of an amiable disposition, but when using a commanding tone, his words told with effect. He was of steady and industrious habits, never flinching from his duty, and in time of action and danger, was cool and calm. . . . [He was] cheerful . . . polite . . . honest and would never talk of his misfortunes. [He] was ready to break up a dispute. He went into the army, saying that he had escaped many dangers, and where it was meant for him to die, there he should die.

Noting that he left a wife and three children "who are now destitute of a provider," the obituarist issued this appeal: "May the citizens of this town now look with pity, and try to aid this distressed widow and her family."

His family never recovered from destitution. Almira, his widow, was granted a pension of $8 a month. When she died in 1912, her son returned her uncashed pension check (which had been increased in amount over the years) with this note: "[My mother] was a great care and expense as she had a cancer, and not money enough to bury her with—so if it would be possible to let me have this money, it would be a great favor."

Worth, George G., private. Age: 20. Occupation: sailor.

He was among those enlisted and mustered by Lieutenant George Nelson Macy on July 18, 1861. Living at the time of his enlistment in Siasconset (then a fishing village on Nantucket's eastern shore), Worth had made one whaling voyage and had worked at a hotel before the war.

He drowned while attempting to cross the Potomac River in the panic that followed the rout of Federal troops at the battle of Ball's Bluff on October 21, 1861. His comrade, Albert B. Holmes, remembered that day:

> Worth and myself went to the river Potomac together—that we were ordered to swim the river, that he said he was going to put in, and he requested me to follow him—I told him that I should go further up the river, which I did and swam over to the other side. There is no doubt that he attempted to swim the river and was drowned. . . . I know that he was a good swimmer having been brought up with him in the Village of Siasconset, on the coast of the Atlantic Ocean, and having made a whaling voyage with him in the Ship Hero of Nantucket. . . ."

Worth's body was recovered at Georgetown, D. C., on November 3. Shortly afterward his father received the following letter:

Georgetown Nov 25 1861

Mr Worth

Sir:

At the request of Mr. Whitney I write to inform you of the particulars of the finding and burial of your son George Gideon Worth. In the first place I will tell you who the parties are. Three of us are seamen, Mr. Wilbert Clary of Gardner, Maine, Mr. Charles Harris of Connecticut and myself a Canadian. We board with the fourth party, Mr. Canning a resident of this place. On Sunday the 3rd of Nov, knowing that the river had risen some twenty or thirty feet we went down to the bank to look at it. While there we saw several bodies float down the stream but we had no boat and could not get them. With a long pole we succeeded in getting hold of one and hauling him ashore which it seems was your son. We got him out upon the bank in a sheltered place and examined his person and pockets. We found no wounds upon him and consequently supposed that his death was wholly caused by drowning. In his pockets we found, a *letter*, a *pocket book*, an *ambrotype*, a pocket handkerchief, a *fine comb* & *a rifle plug.*

The envelope was gone and the lower corner of the letter also, but upon a little piece of paper was written Geo Gideon Worth. We could do nothing that evening because we supposed that the law required a inquest, but the Magistrate of this town informed us that such was not the case, and farther he said that he would come the next day and bury him properly. I went to Georgetown leaving my comrades to see to it. It was that day that I wrote to Mr. Whitney. Upon returning home I found the Magistrate had not been near the place and we proceeded to bury him ourselves. We made no great display but we did it decently.

> "Slowly and sadly we laid him down
> From the field of his fame fresh & gory
> We carved not a line, we raised not a stone
> But left him alone in his glory"

Although he was a stranger to us we felt sad when we covered his remains. We feel for your loss, Sir, but he died in a noble cause. Thousands of families have been equally afflicted with your own, but a feeling of Pride should swell their hearts when they think that their sons have fallen in defense of that glorious principle which their forefathers bled and died to establish. LIBERTY.

You will find the Ambrotype very much defaced. I will forward them immediate with the exception of the rifle plug, which with your permission I will keep and bring it there myself some day perhaps, as it is too heavy to send by mail. If sir there is any thing else you would like to know that I have omitted, I will inform you cheerfully.

Yours truly,

Ralph Garratt.

Worth's body was eventually returned to Nantucket and is buried on the south side of Prospect Hill Cemetery.

Wyer, William M., private. Age: 26. Occupation: shoemaker. Height: 5' 6". Hair: Black. Comp: light. Eyes: grey.

He enlisted and mustered the same day as Josiah F. Murphey on August 12, 1862, and joined the regiment at Alexandria on August 29. He was taken sick in December 1862, and was discharged for disability on April 3, 1863, for "chronic diarrhea of four months standing."

On December 16, 1863, he reenlisted in Company F, 2nd Massachusetts Cavalry. He was discharged on July 7, 1865, probably for expiration of service.

He returned to Nantucket after the war. In 1866 he was examined by a local physician and found to be "still afflicted with chronic diarrhea and is unable to earn a support for himself & family." He joined the local chapter of the G.A.R. in 1866 during its first incarnation.

ON THE SUBJECT OF THE MEN OF NANTUCKET who had stood at Antietam, Fredericksburg, Gettysburg, the Wilderness, and all the other bloody battlefields, the chairman of the Nantucket board of selectmen wrote to the Commonwealth of Massachusetts on December 13, 1865, in response to an inquiry from Adjutant General William Schouler, who had requested information on the circumstances of returned servicemen:

Sir:

In reply to your circular letter of the 9th inst, relative to the conduct of returned soldiers, I have to say that so far as relates to Nantucket, we have no cause for complaint; We have quite a number of this class with us at the present time, many of them without employment, but we have not observed that their morals have depreciated since they enlisted in their country's cause, or that they are not as good men today, and as peaceful citizens, as before entering the service. We have not a single case of crime to record against any returned soldier.

Very Respectfully.
Your obedient servant,
Joseph Mitchell 2nd
Chairman, Selectmen